Angel Works

Angel Works

Soaring From Abuse To Love, Forgiveness and Enlightenment

Barbara Anne Rose

BALBOA.
PRESS
A DIVISION OF HAY HOUSE

ISBN: 978-1-4525-5445-7 (sc)
ISBN: 978-1-4525-5446-4 (hc)
ISBN: 978-1-4525-5444-0 (e)

Library of Congress Control Number: 2012911435

Balboa Press books may be ordered through booksellers or by contacting:

Balboa Press
A Division of Hay House
1663 Liberty Drive
Bloomington, IN 47403
www.balboapress.com
1-(877) 407-4847

Because of the dynamic nature of the Internet, any web addresses or links contained in this book may have changed since publication and may no longer be valid. The views expressed in this work are solely those of the author and do not necessarily reflect the views of the publisher, and the publisher hereby disclaims any responsibility for them.

The author of this book does not dispense medical advice or prescribe the use of any technique as a form of treatment for physical, emotional, or medical problems without the advice of a physician, either directly or indirectly. The intent of the author is only to offer information of a general nature to help you in your quest for emotional and spiritual well-being. In the event you use any of the information in this book for yourself, which is your constitutional right, the author and the publisher assume no responsibility for your actions.

Any people depicted in stock imagery provided by Thinkstock are models, and such images are being used for illustrative purposes only.
Certain stock imagery © Thinkstock.

Printed in the United States of America

Balboa Press rev. date: 7/31/2012

To my children and to all of you.

Seek the Truth and you will find it but then it will trouble you, but through the trouble you will be set free.
—Jesus Christ

ILLUSTRATIONS

CONTENTS

Foreword

Knowledge is something everyone should continually seek. One can never have enough and should never be satisfied with what he or she has already acquired. My own life has been spent constantly learning new things.

Until a few years ago, I had thought of myself as a pretty good learner. I have an excellent memory and am able to make connections between the information I have learned and any practical and useful applications it might have. I realized that I didn't know everything, but I felt that if I needed to know it, I could learn it. That was my problem; there was so much I needed to learn, and I didn't even know it. I had only learned things that I felt had a practical purpose. Essentially, skills that would make me a good living. I knew people who studied other things such as philosophy and spirituality, but I felt I didn't have time for such things.

Then I met Barbara. She was starting a new chapter in her life. She would talk about her dreams, her visions, and how her visions would become realities. She accomplishes this through her belief in herself and her desire to help others achieve their own dreams and make their own visions a reality.

She introduces to those who are open and free a world in which all of the beautiful possibilities can be realized by all of us. Those who are fortunate enough to meet her in person realize this instantly. She has a natural ability to recognize areas within us that need nurturing and healing.

Barbara has the ability to seemingly focus all that is good in the universe upon you with her touch, her voice, and her presence. It is the creator, the protector, and the teacher within her that guides her and that will teach you to become aware of the spirit within yourself.

Within the pages of this book, you will find that she is a goddess and an angel and that she is continually driven to achieve her dreams. How you choose to use her words will be up to you. You should approach it with your mind open to hers. She is the giver, and you are the receiver.

As you read and see her world through her eyes, reflect upon your own memories, your own past, and your own future. Consider what you might have done differently in the past if you had been able to see with the clarity that Barbara has seen. Consider what you will do differently as you begin to see with that clarity for your future. You have taken the first step by reading this book.

Whatever your own personal dreams are, the words and thoughts she has shared will help them become a reality. Once you understand that there is more to this life than that which meets the eye, then your own thoughts will guide you through your own path to your dreams.

—David Lawrence
A long time friend and client.

PREFACE

My reasons for undertaking this work started back on the day I can remember sitting on my parents' kitchen floor at two years of age. I was shy in my ways, but I always remained tuned in to myself and my surroundings. Being aware of the people around me and the energy they held in their bodies and in the spaces of the world in which they lived, I would become aware of me and how I acted and reacted to them and to my own self.

Even though I may not have always been aware of all things consciously, it was like I could feel things happening at a deeper subconscious level. I was aware of not fully being aware, knowing that something deeper was at play in me, in others, and in this world in which I lived. As I became more *awake*, my spiritual gift of sight was developing/increasing. Because of this it happened more frequently.

Imagine this: We are all flowers. The flower knows everything it needs to know in order to fully flourish at its peak. The flower knows all of its petals. The flower knows if it has thorns or not. It knows all of the different colors it can possess. It knows the seeds within the middle of its core. Its seeds are its soul spirit, which is an energy in and of itself. The body of the flower knows it has this soul spirit. They are aware of each other. Each knows it has independence. The flower knows it works together, separately, and synergistically with its core—the seeds. The power of one does not overtake the other. The flower respects and loves each of its parts unconditionally, each part with its own integrity.

The sum of all of these parts makes the flower, as a whole, complete and beautiful. A powerful flower with tremendous possibilities. Not one single part of the flower has a negative attitude toward another, for if it did, the flower would surely die. The flower knows not to possess negativity. It doesn't have negativity. It knows not of it. It already knows the beauty and love it possesses; it is always in a loving state, always joyful and always peaceful. It is what it is.

Now imagine someone comes along and plucks it out of its garden, pinching its nerve. Now the flower knows it is not alone. It knows there are other things out there that can cause it harm. It may get knocked around here and there, hear nasty words, or feel negative vibrations from the person handling it. Maybe the person who yanked it out of the ground slapped it around, carelessly threw it on the counter, or did not feed it immediately with loving, kind words. Maybe now this flower has come into a home with a family. The flower knows the love it has within itself; it feels it and still has it, but the flower wonders, *What has just happened?* The flower wonders what kind of life it will live among these people who call themselves humans. The flower doesn't feel the humanity in the humans. It just feels sadness.

We are all flowers. Once pure in spirit and pure in love, we once knew all things good. My research is my life. The experiences I have had throughout my life have shaped me.

Ever since I was a child, I knew I would be called to do something that would affect people with my love and light. I am now here, giving to you. This is why I have undertaken this thing called life.

I give my sincere thanks to everyone at Balboa Press who has helped me bring this book to fruition.

I would also like to thank a dear friend and colleague, Richard D. Smith, for spending so many of his timeless hours reading and offering his words of wisdom. I thank my friend David Lawrence for writing the foreword to this book and for his belief in me and in the writing of this book.

I thank my children for loving me, supporting me in this work, and for being the beautiful people they are.

I thank my mom for giving birth to me. I am grateful that she's always wanted me to be happy in whatever I chose to do, personally and professionally. I thank my father for the times when he pushed me in life and when he said the words *I love you.* I thank him for instilling in me determination.

Lastly and most importantly, I give my forever humble gratitude to Angels of Light. And I thank myself for allowing me to be open to receiving such divine guidance. Without the Angels of Light, this book would not exist.

In humble gratitude,
my love and light to all,
—Barbara Anne Rose

INTRODUCTION

I write my life story for anyone who seeks to know his or her own light. I write my life story to give inspiration, not just for women who have survived sexual abuse or any form of domestic violence, but to help all—men and women, young and the old—to not only know all of who you are but to also help inspire you to change. In changing your own self enough, you can then inspire others to change.

My life has had its ups and downs, just as yours has. This book is about love. It is about life. It is about beating the odds when the odds don't even look to be in your favor. It is a story of never giving up on your dreams. We are each given so much, but how many of us really use what we have inside us to pursue purposefully, energetically, and passionately?

This book starts in the beginning, with me in a meeting of divine intervention. I will take you on a journey that happened before I was born. We will soar together through the scary times I encountered with a loved one to the joy of finding the father of my children. You will experience with me the downfall of my marriage and the power and freedom of moving forward. You will travel with me as I embrace success and overcome obstacles.

I invite you to experience with me the highs and lows through life and deaths of loved ones. You will find moments when I travel back and forth from one place to another, one time frame to another, sinking deeper into the depths of the many events that have happened in my life. I travel from my childhood to my teens, through marriage and children, through divorce and death. I take you full circle. I will talk about God, our Creator, my prayers, and answers to prayers. Feel, see, and learn powers of angelic light dispersed throughout the book. I also provide observations and exercises for your use.

This is not just a story of events I have lived, but rather it is a story of victorious survival. May you feel every emotion. May you laugh, cry, vent, and feel all emotions that run through your body. Feel the thoughts that go through your mind. Feel your heart beat, your ears open, your eyes widen, your lips part in wonderment. I want you to feel with all your being.

Enjoy this journey with me. I am excited to share it with you. I would love to hear your feedback once you finish reading. Hearing from my readers inspires me to work more, help more, and be more of all of who I am.

I want to give thanks to you, my dear friend, as you read this story about my life. What pleasures. Be everything to yourself, for I wish you blessings and everlasting love.

Let's go!

In October 2009, a Native American man reached out to me online to book a massage session. The moment I saw his request come through, I was excited to say yes, so I did. The reason I was excited was that he was an American Indian. I also have American Indian blood from my Cherokee heritage. I called this man, and we talked. He let me know that if I liked, he would perform a ceremony on me after I gave him a massage. I eagerly accepted.

It had been only recently, just a couple of months prior to this man's e-mail, that I had called out to the universe to send me someone in human form to help me. I knew I needed help from a man to release negative energies attached to me by my father and ex-husband. I had great excitement inside, knowing that something powerful would happen on the day of our meeting. I had been ascending as much as I could on my own by reading many books, meditating, doing my own thing, and looking for people or groups of people who thought the same way I did. I had been practicing the law of attraction, but it was deeper for me than that. Even though everyone I had met had served me in some way, I knew in my soul, in my spiritual being, that what I was searching for was deeper. I searched for and wanted truth—universal truth. I wanted not something someone claimed as truth, but *real* truth. I felt there was a much bigger picture than what was being presented to me.

As I would soon find out, this "man" would be the one to supply this truth, and I was healed along the way. I cannot go into details of how the ceremony happened because that is sacred between me and my healer. What I can say is that I am so very glad I went through all of the ceremonies and teachings over the course of the years he has been teaching me. I have grown and learned so much throughout my years prior, but once I met him, my growth and learning expanded, and my love for myself and others really moved forward.

This particular quest began in 2006. I was ecstatic about having a place of my own. I'd been living with my parents for five years since the separation from my husband in 2001. I had waited for this dream of having my own place for five years. I came to my townhouse as a single mom with three children. We had been married for fifteen years and had three children together, two boys and one girl. Our marriage had been cut short on April 26, 2001, prior to our fifteenth anniversary and one week after my thirty-sixth birthday. I had gone through many trials and tribulations, joys and sorrows. It was the end of a chapter in my life; I was ready to begin another.

I was now in my townhouse and had a career that paid decent money, and I felt confident with where I was heading in life. Having my own place was a big deal for me because it was a first. I was so used to having someone care for me for so long—parents or a husband—that I was now ready to take care of myself. It was a new step, a gain of more freedom and self-confidence. I had always felt I would meet this day of being on my own sometime, so it felt sweet. I wanted more for myself spiritually, so I searched at different churches. Some were close by, and others were farther away. Each had its own place in my growth, but none of them fit right or felt right for me. There seemed to be something missing or something more my soul felt wasn't there. Deep within me I felt I knew truths these churches did not know.

I went to different churches off and on for years, with breaks in between that I spent meditating and reading. I did things and read books or watched movies I felt drawn to at the time. Some resonated with me; some I felt were not in tune with higher angelic powers. I found I received more from my own studies and meditation than from any church I belonged to over the course of my life. I felt God inside me. I was sensing, hearing, seeing, and feeling that things were off when it came to spirituality and when it came to universal truth, so I continued my search from internal guidance.

At one point I even had regular visits with a psychic. I thought I needed to see someone to tell me much of what I already knew about my own life. The psychic told me things of which I was already aware, but for some reason I felt I needed her to clarify what I already knew. I didn't trust myself enough. I realized I didn't trust my own inner guidance and knowing. It was during this time that I called out to God, to the universe for someone to hear me and be sent my way. I knew no human could take off the negative attachments I had formed.

My mind, body, and emotions were driven by my own self-hatred. I was tired of my issues. All the turmoil and hurt I had inside of me over my father and ex-husband had caused much anxiety. I wanted to release my issues in the healthiest way—spiritually, emotionally, and physically. Because I knew I had much love to give to another, I was open to look at my spirit with an open mind and a pure heart. I knew how worthy of being focused upon I was, so I focused on me. I loved me enough to do the work. I wanted to be in love with me. I wanted to know it and feel it deep inside without crying myself to sleep almost every night.

I felt and thought that I was damaged goods, that no man would find me worthy enough or value me enough or even love me enough. I wanted a life partner so badly it hurt. I had one big hole in my heart. I thought I needed a man to fill it. I waited and waited and waited and was only partially filled when men came along and stepped into shoes too big for anyone to fill. I knew I wasn't supposed to need a man. But I wanted one. I am sure I realized on a deeper level that it was me who needed to fill me. It was me who needed to find me so I could fill myself with great love. This was a love only spirit could fill. I was afraid I wouldn't be able to accomplish this. It was a vicious cycle in my life. Like a dog chasing its tail, around and around I went, going everywhere and nowhere at the same time.

I am glad I persevered, pushing myself to move forward through difficult times. I would not be where I am now if I hadn't. I also knew that somehow, in some way, I was here to help people through the work I was to do. I wasn't quite sure how, but I believed in listening to my inner guide, my surroundings, people, animals, and nature.

I had many visions as a child, and still do, in which I could see parts of my future. They were prophetic, some would say. In these visions I saw myself as an enlightened being. I wondered how it would happen, what I would go through to learn even more. I wanted that more than anything. I knew I would need to reach this place before a life partner would not only come into my life but stay.

When I met this *man*, an American Indian man who said he could help me, I told him of my wanting, of my needing, and of my asking for assistance from a man who was not man as we know it to help heal me. He told me who he really was, and I believed. I trusted and wanted to surrender to this divine being. There were many times I had difficulty surrendering. My fear got in the way. There were times when I should have listened more carefully and heeded this divine being's advice, but I didn't. My ego got in the way of my healing. Fear was at the root of it. I feared I was incapable of the work required. I worried about not performing well.

I found out throughout this journey that I was living in many boxes. There were many times when I said mean things to this divine being. I didn't listen to him. I ended up running away from grace for six months. Being away from him for this length of time and allowing my ego to get in the way of his teachings, I pretty much lead my life the way I wanted, caring but not caring about what he was teaching me about universal truth. He reminded me that this was not his truth or a cultural truth but rather universal truth.

Sometime later I was working out at the gym when my inner being spoke and said, "Call him." I called him up, and we talked. I saw, of course, that he had been right all along. I humbly asked for forgiveness and his help. Yes, there continued to be times when it was difficult for me to accept some of the things he said, but I hung in there. I needed to learn to trust and surrender.

Some may say it takes time to trust, and I agree to a point, but with this man—this individual divine being—to hold out and wait to trust would have done me more of a disservice. Sometimes we need to jump in with both feet and do it. We need to stop talking and giving excuses and instead put actions behind our words. It can be difficult at times, especially when we have been so used to thinking, doing, and behaving in certain ways all of our lives. But there comes a point when we need to become more serious about our spirit. We need to be pushed in the right direction—a firm, yet gentle push to take ourselves out of ourselves. To take ourselves out of the boxes and walls we have created over the course of our lives.

I will admit that there were times when I didn't particularly like everything he said. There were times I ran away, so to speak, because I didn't want to believe his words. The fact is that I had a hard time admitting to myself that his words were true. I wanted to be right. His words were about men I had dated. I had asked him his thoughts about certain individuals. I spoke of personal matters between me and the individuals I had been with. My Indian friend, he could see, hear, and "know" things. I didn't like what he said because I had loved and cared for the men I had been seeing.

I have always been a woman who has given one hundred percent of herself. Not only had those men not been right for me, but they didn't, couldn't, or wouldn't give one hundred percent of themselves. I would put a wall up and continue being with those men anyway, even though I knew on a soul level it wouldn't work. I just wanted a man to be beside me and with me, to comfort me, touch me, love me, and support me in my well-being. They just couldn't do that. Nor should they. I knew I had to be the one to love me unconditionally. I had to support myself and rely on me. For we are the only ones we can ever rely on. Never another person.

My Indian friend, coach, and healer helped me so much more. He helped me know more. He helped me understand more. He helped me understand, learn, and know more about all of life, not just relationships. He helped me understand more about unconditional love. We humans think we know what unconditional love is. We think we know what divine love is. But we really do not. My beautiful, beautiful friend has never given up on me. He is a friend who has allowed me space when I needed it. He is a friend who let me have my space when I left. He let the circle turn. He is a friend who is not afraid to tell me like it is—the truth. The truth may be troubling to us when we first hear it, but through those troubling feelings, with an open heart and mind, we can be set free.

Jesus Christ is also a close friend. However, despite what he went through to teach us truth, many of us still do not know all the truth teachings of Jesus. We humans have our own perceptions of much, if not all, of what Jesus said, for we were not physically with him. We did not live with Jesus for him to give us a more complete understanding. And that is okay. We all have free will to accept and not accept, to do and not do, to be and not be, to think and not think, to believe and not believe. But our Creator has given us … *us*. Our Creator has given us the same spirit as Jesus. The truth resides within us, for we have all been made in the same image. There is no one greater than the other. All of us have the same white light—our great knowing. It is in there, deep down inside, lost, and forgotten.

We all need a little help now and again. We still need guidance, healers, and coaches to give us a little push forward in the right direction. How do you know who to go to? Who to believe in? What to believe as you search for your guide, your true friend? There are real angels on this earth that are here in human form to help us. We need to open our eyes, our ears, and our hearts in order to see, hear, and recognize when this help comes to us. We ask, and they present themselves. I asked, and I received. My eyes were opened, and I saw. My ears were opened, and I heard. My lips were opened, and I spoke. He heard and spoke to me that October day. My healer is an angel in the human form of an American Indian man. I shall call him my Angel Bearer of Light.

This is the beginning of the story of my own enlightenment. I will go through parts of my life for you so that you will see I am just a normal person like you. I too have had my troubling times. I too have had pain. I too have lost loved ones. I too have suffered at the hands of someone else's demons. I too have given birth to new life. You will see that I am a lot like you.

As you read my story, you may find that some of my life events are similar to yours. Other pieces of my life may not be. Read, hear, and listen through it all, as I hope you will see, hear, and value the lessons I have experienced. Keep an open heart. Keep an open mind. I want you to be a willing vessel of light and love. I want you to see just how beautiful you are. I want you to see how you can have all of your desires, dreams, wants, and needs met. I want you to find *you*. You are a light being. I want you to see that you are love, that you are joy, that you are peace, and that you are worthy of everything good. I will do my best to inspire and motivate you to know who you really are and to know how to be who you really are at any given moment. I want you to be patient with yourself. I want you to not give up on you or others. I want you to know, *really* know, just how very precious you are.

Each of us is born perfect. We do not come into this life with sin as many have been taught growing up. This book is not about bashing anyone or anything. It is about taking you back to the source of who you really are. It is about going back to learning the basic laws of life, the simple laws the universe gives us. The laws our Creator has given us allow us to have as we choose. I use the word *Creator* because we are the cause of creation. We are beings of light energy in its purest form. Our light was created for us thousands upon thousands of years ago.

Let's start this process of creation now and move on to live exemplary lives.

CHAPTER I

Before My Birth

Remembrance

I remember being born. I remember feelings, sensations, and movements I made within my mother's womb. I remember feeling her love, the love she had for me, her child—the small, intricate baby girl growing bigger and bigger every day inside the jellylike fluid of the amniotic sac. Oh what a feeling to be able to stretch and swim and move all over within my mother's womb with no worries.

I will never forget the day in late September of 2008 when I felt the love my mother had for me, her unborn child. It all started one night with the moon almost full and a slight breeze in the air. It was a mild fall day, one of those days you just aren't sure what to do: eat, love, pray, or—heck—even all three. Besides, it was just me alone in my house. I could do what I wanted. I loved my freedom.

So there I was, deciding to walk upstairs to my bedroom for my evening meditation. As I walked up the steps, I felt good. I felt a sense of accomplishment, a sense of tranquility, peace, and contentment. I loved my life. I had painted my room, splashing green everywhere. The way the color lay on the walls took me away to other places. It was a soothing color.

That darn crack in the wall. How did that get there? I thought to myself. *I need to call maintenance. They take forever sometimes. Oh well, I do what*

I have to do. I was in my bedroom now, which was not much bigger than a twelve-by-fifteen box. At least I had a full bathroom to shower in and a cute, small walk-in closet. My cathedral ceiling was twelve feet high. A good selling point, I thought—the successful, professional business woman that I was—even though the townhouse I was in at the time was only a rental. Love knows no end.

I sat cross-legged on my bed, looking into the dresser mirror I had held onto from my marriage. I focused on my lit white candle, readying myself for my daily meditation. I use no music—just me, myself, and I with my candle. The candle had come from a friend of mine. It was a blessed candle. She had it blessed in the church she was a part of, and she had also given it her own personal blessing. I had thanked her for that. It was special to me, and I always felt good when lighting it and meditating with it.

This night felt like a special night. I just knew it. I felt it. I could *see* it. My eyes gazed upon the lit white candle, watching the flame moving from side to side, getting bigger and smaller. I noticed all the ways the flame expanded and grew, gently swaying to the right and then ever so lovingly to the left. There were constant, beautiful changes of this loving energy, this force of light and power that I loved and embraced. I took it all inside me.

My hands lay on my knees, palms up, and I closed my eyes softly, gently, and with care. I breathed in and out, in and out, in and out, going down inside of myself. I first noticed my own quietness and then the quietness around me and my home. Everything felt and was so still. I took another nice breath down within. I saw beautiful colors—purple, yellow, blue, green, violet, red, pink, and orange. The colors of the rainbow, I noticed. *Ah*, I felt as I soaked them all inside me. I always started in my heart and then progressed down to my root chakra. Then I directed my energy all the way back up and into my head and heart again. I loved my mom. I loved how she read bedtime stories to me and my little sister. It was lovely and comfortable. I enjoyed listening to my mom's voice. It felt good and reminded me of the times when I was in her womb. Yes, I remember the times inside of her, me as a baby growing and being nourished, loved, and cared for. I remember the feeling of the fluid surrounding me like an ocean of waves. I even remember hearing other voices coming from outside of her. Pleasant voices, raised voices, laughter, tears, strength, and anger. Sometimes I heard my mother and a man arguing. I wondered, *Is this my dad?* I hoped not, but if it was, then it was, and I would be okay. I would know what to do and how to handle myself. I would know how to be and not be.

Suddenly I felt myself going back in time as a small, wee child—a baby. I was inside my mother! I felt me! I saw and realized all of this consciously in my adult body, but at the same time I was also consciously aware of me, the infant child inside of my mother's womb. I felt me, the tiny baby growing. I felt the love my mother had for me. I felt her fluid. I felt the fluid around me, floating around, and I felt safe. I felt comforted. I felt beautiful. I felt good. It was so beautiful to feel all of this as an infant, but it was also beautiful because there I was, an adult, experiencing it and having this memory. *I am here. I am free. I love you, Mommy. Thank you for loving me.*

As I was in this state of knowing of life, I felt that there was so much going on all of the time all around me, all around us, all around the world. I anxiously awaited my own birth into the physical world. And so I waited with love in my heart, with love I carried in my eyes, my ears, my hands, and all of me for all of you. I lay in peace.

Being Born

It was a hot day in August 1964. The heat outside intensified as the stifling temperatures rose, burning the hairs in my mother nostrils. Blades of the thick green grass were scorched from lack of rain. The air was thick with humidity. I sensed and felt the outside. What intensity of senses I had while I lay inside my mother's womb. It was good and well inside her flesh. The fluid surrounding me protected me, enveloping my body. What comfort I felt, a sense of peace and tranquility.

I was so tiny inside of her then, yet I felt, saw, and knew things that can't be explained in human scientific terms. It was okay that no one would believe me, as I already knew there would be so many happenings in the life I was about to be born into. So many life lessons to embrace and learn, so many trials to work through, overcome, and experience. I already knew it would all be for the good and benefit of my soul and of so many other souls yet unknown and unheard, but they are there. They would know when the time was right, when the time was near to seek truth for themselves. We were all there to seek and know truth. I was glad for my spirit to enter into this body, growing and being nourished inside this mother of mine.

My mother was a beautiful woman with jet-black hair. Her personality shined through her eyes, her face, her body, and her smile. She had such great eyes of a lovely spirit. She told me I had older brothers and sisters, that I was her eighth child. The two she carried inside her before me lasted for a short period of time, one boy and one girl. She had miscarried. "It is okay," she informed me. "Everything happens for a reason."

I loved my mother, and I knew she loved me. She talked so sweetly and so gently and with much care. A beautiful woman my mother was. As I lay inside her, listening to her talk to me, feeling her steps walk us forward around the yard filled with sweet flowers, I smelled roses. All the colors of the rainbow were there. The grass blade tips might have been scorched from the lack of rain that summer brought, but I knew and saw lots of green. The tall trees around the house where we lived were connected to us. I saw a swing set that my older brothers and sisters played on.

My mom told me one of my sisters, the one born before me, was slow to speech. She told me that doctors were doing tests on her to find out what might be wrong, why she didn't function at the normal rate of a four-year-old child. *I am sorry, Mommy, that you don't know what is wrong with my sister. The doctors will find out. At least she's healthy. She is so pretty too. I love her, Mommy. Don't worry. I will help you when I am old enough. I promise I will. Daddy will help you too, won't he, Mommy?* I thought my daddy loved my mommy. I heard them sometimes when they didn't speak nicely to each other. They didn't know what was wrong with my older sister, but they thought it was Rett syndrome.

Daddy was excited for the birth yet to come. I hoped that he would like me. *Will I be a good enough daughter for him?* I could already feel and tell that he got really angry at Mommy sometimes. *Daddy, don't hurt Mommy. She loves you and is doing all she can to make dinner the way you want. Why do you have to be so mean to her? You're not the only one who loves her and lives here,* I thought as I lay within my mother's womb.

I saw my brothers and sisters. She had to take care of them too. *Stop yelling at her. Please stop, Daddy. Don't you know what you are doing? Can't you see? Why do you never listen? You are not listening with your heart. You're just hearing her. Well, now I know I'm going to have to work hard just to prove myself to you. Oh, why do I have to have a daddy like this? At least I know my new mommy loves me. Not like my past life. Well, I am glad I am done with that one. Hey, it was fun when I got older and gave no care. So why am I in this one? Yes, that's right, to do good in this life. How is it going to be with a daddy who doesn't even really like Mommy that much? All he seems to do is hurt her emotionally. How does Mommy put up with it? Well, Mommy, I'll love you enough for all of us. I won't let you down. I will do everything in my power to do good and be good. I'll be a perfect little girl and love you back. I'll snuggle with you and kiss your forehead. I'll run my hands through your hair. You're so pretty, Mommy. Doesn't Daddy think you're pretty?*

As time passed and I grew, I got bigger inside my mother. It felt like I was almost ready to be born. There was not as much room in there for me to move. The only direction I felt the need to go was down. It was kind of hard, but I could feel an opening, so I moved myself closer. I thought I was hurting my mother, that it didn't feel very good for her, but she was anxious for me to come out. I knew she was! And I was anxious to see my mother face-to-face.

A new life to begin. I didn't remember much about all other lives I'd lived. It was all just a blur. It didn't matter too much now anyway, for I was there in this life for a reason. *I will make good and do good for myself and others. Yes, it does feel good. Here we go.* I moved down closer to the entrance of the outside world. I could push out to stretch myself more. *I am coming, Mommy! Here I come, brothers and sisters! Can you not wait for me to arrive? I can't wait to see all of you. Hi, Daddy! Hi, Mommy! Wow, I am out. It feels cold. Someone's holding me, carrying me over to somewhere, laying me down on a cold physical thing. Okay, you can take me off now and give me to my mom. Now this feels better. I'm wrapped up nice and cozy and warm in a blanket. Thank you.*

I felt them lay me down in my mother's arms. She was nurturing me, kissing me, and touching me. Touch felt good. The love felt good. As I nursed on my mother's breast, the warm, sweet milk tasted divine. She didn't do this for long, as I remember later being bottle-fed. Mommy's breast was better, sweeter and more real. Like angel medicine. I liked the connection.

Going home, my daddy drove us in a big blue Buick. He was happy then, but he was not always happy. Something was different about him. I wasn't sure what to think. It just felt off. We arrived home, and all my brothers and sisters were there. My aunt Fran was there, helping my mom out with the other children. She was kind of goofy. One by one my siblings came around to see me, their baby sister, Barbara Anne. That was what they named me—Barbara Anne. I thought it was a pretty name. A very pretty name. I was tired. It was time for me to sleep.

CHAPTER 2

The Beginning Years

1968—Three Years of Age

At three years of age in 1968 my family lived in a house in Baltimore, Maryland. We were going to be moving to a brand-new house. Everyone was excited and eager to see it. I wondered which room would be the one me and my younger sister would share.

I remember being sick. I was three years old, up late, worried about my swing set. We were going to be moving, and I wanted to make sure my swing set was coming with us. I was not going to go to bed until I saw with my own eyes proof that my swing set was coming too. I sat on my mommy's lap in the kitchen with my dad and my older brother, Jim. I hadn't felt well that day. I didn't know how the process would go, how my swing set was going to be transported from the house I lived in to the one we were moving to. I ended up getting sick all over my mom. When I got off of her lap to walk over to the kitchen sink, I stepped on a tack, and I cried. As my dad held me up by my arms, my brother held me by my feet and pulled the tack out of my left foot. What a relief. My brother, he knows how to pull a tack out of a foot really well. *Thank you, Jim!* I exclaimed in my mind. Then Mommy held me again, and I snuggled myself next to her bosom. Soon afterward, I saw the shadow of a moving truck on the kitchen wall, followed by the truck itself. Yea, it was there! Once I saw

7

this, I relaxed, feeling happy and relieved. Now I would be able to sleep restfully. Interesting, some of the things we remember.

In 1968 when we reached our new home in Delaware, one of my older sisters bolted out of the car, sprinting forward in the hopes of claiming her room. With bubbly glee of eagerness and joy, she suddenly found that the front door was locked. Seeing an open window, she slyly squeezed herself through. She was silly on this warm day in her short shorts.

It was in this house at the age of four that I would ask my mom about getting my ears pierced. I wanted it badly, and I was not about to give up. I asked my mommy several times, imploring her to let me get my ears pierced. I *knew* I wanted this. Two months later, she obliged to my request and made an appointment with the doctor. Yes, back then that's what we did. Can you imagine doing that now, calling a doctor to put a hole in your ears for earrings? My mom picked out a set of her gold-plated hoop earrings that I would wear for the next few years. I may have been shy and reserved, but I was determined. Once my mind was made up about something, there was no stopping me.

The day of my appointment, I wore shorts and a short-sleeved top, looking as cute and adorable as ever with eyes of dark blue, a nose shaped like my mother's, a shy smile, and curls like my dad. I couldn't wait. My mommy warned me ahead of time that the doctor would be using a needle to puncture my earlobes. I heard and understood, but I did not know what it would feel like until the day arrived.

I remember the doctor wanting me to lie down on his table so he could perform the piercing. The first thing he needed to do was mark a dot on each ear with a felt-tip pen where the needle would enter. But every time he got close to me, attempting to mark my ears with the pen, I screamed. Over and over and over again, I fought him off, shaking my head from side to side. I didn't know why I felt the need to scream, and I didn't know it was only a felt-tip pen he had in his hand. He told me to shut up, stop moving, and stop crying. I didn't want to stop. I wanted to fight him off and get him away from me. But my mom wasn't about to leave the doctor's office until it was done, especially after I had told her how badly I wanted my ears pierced. Both he and my mom held me down, and my mom did her best to comfort me while the doctor marked the spots on my ears. From then on, I don't remember much. I must have decided to just lie there and take it when he made the holes with the needle. I was glad when it was over.

Many years later, in 2011, the day before Christmas, my oldest son, his wife, my mom, and I got together for breakfast. My mom and I sat side-by-side while my son and his wife sat side-by-side. During our conversations, the memory of getting my ears pierced came to mind. We weren't even talking about ear piercings, but my mom was expressing to me how she kept losing one of her earrings. She looked at me. I turned my head toward her, looking at her face-to-face, and I saw the small green earring in her left ear—an earring she'd had for as long as I could remember. It brought back the memory of me wanting my ears pierced as a child.

I proceeded to tell her the story about me wanting my ears pierced when I was four. That's all I said. My mom continued to talk of a memory she had of me losing an earring of hers that I had worn back then. She told me that one day when I went to school, I had come home with one of the earrings missing from my ear. Apparently, it had fallen off at some point during the day. I didn't know when or where it had fallen off. She had thought it was lost for good at school.

She went on with the story, telling us how she had found it outside on the sidewalk by our front door. Listening to her talk, I remembered more. I remembered why I had fought so hard that day at the doctor's office, screaming and crying. I had fought back because my father had threatened me, taken advantage of me. At that time, the abuse had still been happening, so no wonder I felt such a threat from a male hovering over me. At least at the doctor's office I could cry and scream. At home I couldn't.

1968—Childhood

On a bright, sunny day in the spring of 1968, I sat quietly on the living room floor of my parents' home. I could hear arguing coming from the kitchen. I didn't like the sound of my parents' stories. I didn't like the sound of their voices. They were not talking prettily to each other.

I had a pretty good life overall, with four sisters and two brothers to take care of me and keep me company. I grew up in a Roman Catholic family, and we attended church every Sunday. That's the way it was. During the service, Daddy stayed home with my older sister who was diagnosed with Rett syndrome. I found out later in life that I'd had two older siblings that died in childbirth. My mom had miscarried the two pregnancies before I came along. I knew I had been meant to be born. All of my brothers and sisters were older than me except one, the younger one being two and half years my junior. A little sister. We were like twins growing up. We always shared a bedroom and did nearly everything together.

As I sat on the wood floor in my parents' living room that day at three years of age, I thought, *What a joy to have a younger sister.* What a cute, adorable, beautiful baby girl she was. As I continued ingesting all the words being exchanged between my mother and father, I wondered about life. I wondered how it would be as I grew up, the things I would do, the places I would see, and what my little body and heart would go through. I told myself, *No one will forget me.*

I felt a deep longing. A place deep inside of me spoke to me and said, "My dear child, you will be successful in everything you do. Don't worry. Just be kind to others and give yourself freely." *Okay,* I thought as I heard and listened to these words. These words didn't come from my parents or from anyone in that room. I heard these words from inside me. *That's interesting,* I thought. *I like this feeling. They are nice to me. Since these words are coming from inside me, there must be another me within this body. There is great joy in feeling this, in knowing this. It must be my spirit. So thank you, spirit.*

Hearing the arguments sitting on the wood floor of my parents' living room floor was the beginning of lessons learned, of trials I would overcome. It was the beginning of dreams started. We are all on a journey together. We are all one in this world called life. Let's do the best we can do in each moment and be kind to people. As a child of three I felt deep within me a knowing to do and be right. It was a time I would come to know there would be many lessons to learn, trials to go through. It was the first day of the rest of my life as I understood it. This was the day that, when I went to bed that night, someone came into my room, my bed and did things to me I wasn't so sure about.

Spirit spoke to me about this too and told me I would be okay. This was the first of many nights and days I would be molested. Most of it happened at night in bed. Sometimes in the shower he would pick me up and do things to me or make me do things to him. I didn't like what was happening, but I couldn't get away. It was forceful. Sometimes the periods of molestation came and went. It wasn't every day, and I am grateful for that. I know my mom loved me, but she didn't understand my quietness, my shyness. No one understood why I retreated at such a young age. I knew, and I wasn't going to tell anyone. I couldn't tell anyone. No one would believe me. I grew up not knowing I was sexually abused by my father until later in life during the course of therapy. I was thirty and had been diagnosed with post traumatic stress syndrome. Abuse is an act of taking away someone's free will in whatever form, whether sexually, spiritually, mentally, or emotionally.

1968—Remembering Abuse

As I lay peacefully in my comfy bed at three years old, all nestled and warm under the covers, after my mommy read me a bedtime story, I fell asleep. Later, I felt someone in bed with me. My eyes were closed, and I wondered, *Who is this?* I woke up and saw my father with his head down where my private parts were. I was frightened and scared, and I wondered why he was lying there with me. Why was he touching me in places that were scary, places I didn't even understand? Why was he touching me? Why were his lips licking me down there, kissing my inner thighs, my legs, the place where I go pee? Why did this feel so weird? How did this feel so weird? I couldn't talk. I couldn't say anything. I wanted to cry, but I was afraid. I was afraid to make any noise. *Mommy, please help me. Mommy, why is Daddy here? Mommy, Mommy, Mommy, why can't you hear me? I need you to save me from this pleasure-pain.*

I didn't like daddy in that moment. *I love daddy, but I hate daddy*, was the thought that ran through my mind. I hated what he was doing to me. *Make him stop. Why aren't you listening to me? Nobody listens to me. I am only a child, and no one lets me talk. They won't believe me. Should I talk? What do I do? He's still licking me, and I really don't like this. Why does he have to touch me like this? I know real daddies don't do this to their little girls. Why me? Leave me alone! I hate you. Do you hear me? I hate you. Oh please, God, make him stop. Do something, God. I'm just a little girl.*

He told me to be quiet, not to say anything to my mother. I cried out for Mommy in my mind, but she couldn't hear me. *Oh, Mommy. I think he is almost done with me. He's just lying there now, not really doing anything but just lying there. Looks like he's sleeping, but oh, there goes his head, moving from one side to the other, looking up at me shortly before he hurries out of the room. Good. Go. Leave me alone and stay away. I know I'm supposed to love you, but I don't. Right now I don't even like myself.* I turned onto my right side, curled my small, little body into the fetal position, and pretended I was back inside my mommy's womb, where everything was soft and warm. It was a place I was loved and protected. Daddy couldn't hurt me there. I could be passive and loved there.

Mommy loved me. I knew she loved me. I remembered the way she felt when I was inside her belly. I remember being in a protective shell. It felt incredibly warm. I could have stayed there forever. *Mommy! Mommy, I love you. Can you feel me now? Can you hear me now? Can you see me now? I want this night to be over, but then I don't. Why do I feel like this? Why do I feel empty inside? Why does my heart hurt? Why do I feel like I just want to die? I'm only three. God, help me. Okay, Mommy, come wake me up and take me away from all this. Did you even know Daddy left your bed to come see me tonight?*

I woke up the following morning, welcomed by my mother's love as she fixed me a bowl of Cheerios with milk and sugar. It tasted good. I relished in my food. I let it take me away for a moment so I didn't have to keep feeling the painful memories. I let my mind and my body go away for the moment. The Cheerios were good, and I liked how Mommy knew how to put on just the right amount of sugar. Just enough sweetness. *Yummy. Hey, yummy and Mommy are almost the same in spelling. Maybe because mommies are yummy?*

As the years went by, I struggled back and forth with the sexual abuse and enjoying the pleasures of food to numb my pain. I used food as a means of coping for many of the years that followed, stuffing down memories and feelings. I later realized that I didn't even know why I ate the way I did. It wasn't until after my marriage and children, throughout the troubles of an unhealthy marriage and going through therapy, that I came to recognize the eating disorder was just a cover to the underlying issue of sexual abuse perpetrated by my father. I had no recollection of sexual abuse until I started receiving therapy in 1995 at the age of thirty.

I can remember some events as far back as the age of two. I remember moments I spent outside eating peanut butter and jelly sandwiches with a glass of cold milk, sitting at a picnic table with my fingers all sticky. My curly hair looked a lot like my dad's. On this day I had a dress on, plaid with white cap sleeves and a white collar. We also had a small children's swimming pool just big enough for a child's slide to play on. I loved playing outside in my pool, going down the slide over and over again on a warm summer's night. I also enjoyed the times we would take walks past the yard and into another yard to go swing. One of my cousins would go with me, and she would push me on the swing. Sometimes two of my other cousins, Robbie and Michael, were with us, and we would all play together, swinging and swimming.

1972—First Birthday Party

My seventh birthday is the first birthday I remember. My sister Lynette was doing all the planning. She was eighteen, and she loved planning those kinds of things. She was so creative and smart. She said she was going to go to college to become a teacher. She was okay, and I was glad she was my sister, but she was too mommy-ish, I guess it was because she was the oldest sister. My brothers hated her and teased her all the time. How annoying that must have been. She was a skinny thing, though, as she pranced herself around in her short miniskirt. It was 1972, and there was free love. My sister Lynette was a hippie.

Well, back to my party. I invited a few friends, boys and girls. The day was perfect, sunny and breezy as we ran around the yard, playing like little girls and boys do. I remember a moment when my daddy had his legs open like a gate for all the kids to scamper through. Round and round we went through his legs. Each time I ran through, I received a little smack on the butt for each of my birthday years. The last two were a little hard; I felt the sting of his hand. *Ouch, Daddy, that's too hard*, I thought. I ignored it and quickly let it go and returned to playing with my friends.

You're not allowed to come to my room tonight, I said in my mind. *I don't want to play those games anymore.* The last time daddy had come to my room was when I was five, but every day and night I wondered if he would come again. I didn't like the things he did to me. I wished I understood him, understood why he had done what he did. *Doesn't Mommy do those things with him? That's what mommies and daddies are supposed to do, not daddies and little girls like me.*

He always told me to be quiet about it, not to say anything, so I didn't. Besides, I was Daddy's little girl. I was the perfect child, the one that could do no wrong. I remember pony rides on his knee too and walking on his feet at dinnertime in the kitchen. Me and my little sister had our own dinner table we ate at.

As the party went on, we were all outside playing games. I liked it when Daddy took us for rides in the tractor. He pulled us in the trailer behind his tractor—you know, the one that cuts grass. That was always fun going for rides around our big yard.

My party ended well that year. My mom made the cake, and of course we had the best ice cream. That year my mommy made chocolate cake with vanilla icing. She made so many things homemade. For presents I got Barbie dolls, paper dolls, and coloring books. I loved all of these things. *Maybe one year my daddy will buy me a horse.* I loved horses and asked every single birthday and Christmas for a live horse, but I never got one.

1972-1976—Elementary School

When I was in elementary school, I was a sweet child. I was always shy, often scared. However, among the unpleasant experiences, there were also many pleasant ones. I have always liked boys, and I have always liked having my hair long. The Native American in me is where that comes from—boys and long hair!

In my second year of elementary school, my mother took me to get my hair cut, and I hated it. It was short. School picture day was coming up, so I think that was why my mom took me for a haircut. To this day, I still remember sitting in the hairstylist's chair.

During recess there were times when everyone played boy-chase-girl or girl-chase-boy. For those of you who are close to my age, you may remember this game. I remember a set of boy twins in my class. I always had my eye on the cuter one. The funny thing was, it was the other twin that liked me. When girl-chase-boy time was called out by my teacher, I chased the good-looking twin. When it was time for boy-chase-girl, the other twin chased me.

Then there was gym class. It was an easy way for me to express my individuality. Not until middle school and high school did that all change. Elementary gym classes were just more fun. We learned cartwheels and back bends. We did jumping jacks and somersaults, forward and backward. I was proud that I could do all of them well. One day in gym class, we were practicing back bends. I lay down on my back to start, placed my hands beside and slightly behind my head, and planted my feet flat on the floor. Then I hiked myself up using the force of my hands and my core to push me up as high as I could go. I went higher than anyone in my class. I went so high that my teacher wanted me to show the principal. Uh oh, now I was nervous, because not only was I going to perform for the principal, but I had a little girl crush on him too. But you know what? I did it. I also showed him how I could do a split. All three ways—a front split and both side splits. I had been practicing these splits every day until I reached the goal of a full split.

My next-door neighbor that lived directly across the street from us taught me these things. She was several years older than me. I liked her, and she liked me. She enjoyed helping younger kids like me and my younger sister do cartwheels and back bends and splits and other such things. She taught me to never give up. She would say to me, "Practice, practice, practice, Barbara, every single day, and one of these days you will be able to complete one." One of my cousins who was in gymnastics also taught me things. They both inspired me.

Another happy event in my childhood was when one of my best friends in elementary school taught me cursive handwriting ahead of my time. She was a year ahead of me in school. I loved being ahead of my grade. Her name was Kelly. When Kelly and I got together to write, she noticed how fast I went.

She asked me, "How do you do that? How do you keep writing one sentence after another without stopping?"

I didn't know how not to. I was just following what came from my mind and transferring it to paper. She seemed amazed at this. To me, it was natural. I thought everyone wrote this way. Later in middle school, I loved reading and writing class. Sometimes our homework involved coming up with a storyline and writing it out. We were also allowed to add illustrations if we wanted. Because I loved to draw, I typically did that too.

I suppose I am a natural born writer? When something is natural, it's not hard. It must be a gift. It is interesting how I would find out later in life everything I experienced would help drive me forward to the many dreams I would pursue. The determination I had when practicing my splits, cartwheels, back bends is what I would use later when putting to use my hands in my work, my writing and my spiritual enlightenment. To put it all together now: my mind, my hands, my spirit, my gift of sight, how all of it plays together. To utilize every part of me in all walks of my life.

We don't often realize how creative we are until someone points it out. Isn't that interesting? We have so many natural abilities, but we don't notice how deeply they can affect us and others around us. We forget or lose track of our own specialness. So let's go back. Step back from yourself and think of the times when you were young. What do you remember enjoying the most? What did you do as a child? What games did you play? Do you remember the dreams you had? Things you wanted to do, places you wanted to go, people you wanted to meet, or cultures you wanted to learn more about, not by just reading about them but by going there?

See how we lose ourselves and create boundaries? How we create our own walls because of the pain and hurt we suffered from others or because of what we think of who or what has hurt us? Maybe we are right. Maybe they are right. We don't always know. We need to know who we are, what we are, and what we want right now, here in this moment.

Stop reading for a moment and think about this. Get out a journal and write your thoughts down. Write down how these thoughts make you feel. Remember who you were. Work on not letting your kids forget who they are. By them being them, let them remind you of who you are. Have fun in healthy, childlike ways. Be a kid again. Go outside and do a cartwheel. Do a headstand or handstand. Do what makes you happy, what sets you free. Just because we are adults doesn't mean we can't play like children sometimes. Sometimes we use our kids as an excuse to go ahead and put our butts on the swing to swing or play in the sandbox or slide down the slide. We don't need to go to an amusement park for good old-fashioned fun. You can still be the responsible adult and play like a child in the same day. Breathe in that life. Let it put a smile on your face.

1978–1983—Preteen and Teen Years

One evening at the age of thirteen when I was in seventh grade, I was in the kitchen helping my mom with dinner. We were making chicken, rice, and green beans.

"Go find your father and let him know dinner is ready," she told me.

We ate dinner every night at 6:00 p.m. sharp. That's the way it had to be—6:00 p.m. *sharp*—so Mom was always expected to have dinner completely ready and on the table by then. If it was five minutes after, Dad would get mad.

My younger sister and I never knew what kind of mood he would be in when he came home from work. Out of all the times I remember him coming home, most days were not pleasant ones. Maybe it was because he was male and his voice was louder. Anytime his voice rose, I felt like I was walking on eggshells. Anxiety, they said that was later in life when I went through therapy. I didn't even know what anxiety meant. I had such a sheltered life.

On the days my dad came home unpleasant, upset, mad, or angry, me and my younger sister would immediately turn off the television set and go upstairs to our room. We usually turned on our radio or listened to one of our records so we couldn't hear his and Mom's words. I didn't like it. It scared me. It was a shame because I wanted to be able to love my dad. I wanted a house of love and care for all. I wanted to feel safe in the home in which I lived. I wanted to express myself and not worry about not being heard or not being hurt verbally or physically.

I was always the quiet one. My younger sister was the one who spoke up. I dared not because I saw what happened to her. I heard my father say harsh words to her. I dared not speak out, for I would be treated the same. I was the princess. I never did anything wrong. I remained the good girl.

When my dad came home and there were pleasantries, I felt safe, so my sister and I felt safe to continue watching TV.

For many years to come, I either overheard discontent between my parents or silence. I only remember seeing affection between them once or twice. One of these times was when I was in the kitchen, watching my mom doing dishes by hand. Her back was turned away from me. She was washing silverware, cups, and plates from a scrumptious meatloaf meal. There had been mashed potatoes and fresh green beans from the garden. I saw my dad walk from his office den into the kitchen and slyly embrace my mom from behind. I saw how she shrugged him away without emotion. I remember thinking that it must have hurt Dad to be rejected by his wife like that. Why would my mom turn away a loving action? I don't remember seeing them affectionate with each other again until their fiftieth wedding anniversary.

Whenever we visited my mom's sister's place, I always saw them as being a close-knit family, kissing, hugging, and embracing one another every time they said their hellos and goodbyes. I was envious of their love and ached in my heart to have this in my life with my parents, brothers, and sisters. I always wanted to know why our family wasn't like that. I knew love and affection were good. Watching my aunt kiss and hug her husband and my cousins kissing and hugging both of their parents every time they said goodbye was a beautiful sight. I wanted that and craved that for my family. It saddened me that we didn't have that kind of love. Did my mom just not like my dad that much?

CHAPTER 3

Young Adulthood

1984—First Memorable Vision

The first day of my first semester of college was beautiful. The sun was gorgeous, and there was a slight breeze in the air. I remember being outside, walking from one building to another. I had just passed a best friend from high school. The moment after passing her, I received a vision. This vision was as clear as the beautiful, sunny day. It remains just as fresh in my mind now as I write this as it was back then.

In this vision, I saw the three children my Creator was going to bless me with. I hadn't even met my future husband yet, but I saw the children I was to conceive years later. I saw two boys and a girl playing together happily in a dining room. I was there in this vision, looking at these children with my own eyes. To help you picture how the vision looked, it was similar to when you are dreaming and you know you are in your dream but you don't see yourself. You can only feel you. You know you are there, and you see what is happening around you like a movie. So as I saw and watched these children, knowing they were mine, I felt eagerness. I felt excited. I felt beautiful. I knew I had this to look forward to. I couldn't tell the children's ages, but I could see that they were all young and close in age. I also could not tell where the girl was in the birth order, whether she first, second, or last. I just knew that there were two boys and a girl.

As far back as elementary school, I had always known I wanted to name my little girl Kelly.

1984—Meeting My Future Husband

I was nineteen and still in my first semester of college when I met the man who was to become my husband. I didn't know what I wanted to do with my life when it came to future employment. All I knew at the time was that I wanted to be married and raise children. I thought of a few things that piqued my interest in terms of employment, but they were limited. Physical therapy, occupational therapy, makeup artist, personal trainer, or hair stylist were a few. Even one of my dad's employees mentioned I would be excellent in occupational therapy. I thought about it and looked into it, but I really didn't think I was smart enough. But I knew I wanted to help change people's lives for the better. Because I wasn't sure what to do, I made it simple for myself and took general studies. In less than a year, I decided to quit college because I had met the man of my dreams.

I grew up Roman Catholic, so I attended church every Sunday. My little sister, my mom, and I would go together. It's weird, but I don't remember any of my other sisters and brothers going with us. In church we did all the usual things Catholics do. Every year the church had a picnic for all the members to get together and relax, have fun, enjoy conversation, eat, and play games. I enjoyed attending this annual event.

In the fall of 1984, the church picnic came around, and I was eager to attend it with one of the other members of the church. We had been eyeing each other for some time by then. At that time I was working as a fitness instructor at an all-women's gym in addition to taking college classes. My boss asked me if I wanted to volunteer to be part of the local fair. I said yes. I, along with one of the other girls I worked with, volunteered together. On the morning of the fair, my friend and I were walking around, looking for where we needed to be. We looked but were not able to find the spot, so we decided to leave. I was actually happy about this because it was too chilly to be sitting in a box, waiting to be dunked into a tub of water. I was eager to get out of there and go meet my date at 1:00 p.m. for the church picnic.

It was September and we had just met just two weeks prior. I had been standing next to my mom in one of the pews in church when I noticed a good-looking guy a few rows in front of us. I wanted to say something to him. Even though I was shy, I knew I wanted to talk to him. I leaned over to my mom and whispered in her ear, "Mom, I think that guy is cute. The one three rows up from us, over to the left, with curly hair."

I liked the frame of his body. He stood tall and confidently. I had been keeping my eye on him for over three months. I could tell he had also been keeping his eye on me. I said to my mom that if he didn't say something the following week, I was going to ask him if he wanted to go to the picnic together. When the next Sunday came around, he wasn't there. I was bummed. Now I had to wait another week. Even though the following week was the day of the picnic, I was still going to ask. I wasn't going to let that hold me back.

The next Sunday rolled around, and I was in church with my mom and sister again. We did our thing—stand and kneel, stand and kneel, and repeated our recitations. Lo and behold, there he was. He was with his mom, and I could sense the other woman with them was his aunt. I found out later that I was right. As church neared its end, I was slightly nervous walking toward him, as he was also walking toward me. He introduced himself with a handshake and his name. I returned the favor, welcoming his handshake and giving him my name.

I didn't hear him clearly so I asked, "What's your last name?" He replied, and I still didn't get it. I politely asked again. He said it one more time. Okay, now I had it. He asked me about going to the picnic together, and I let him know about my other responsibility with the fair.

"If you would like to meet me here in the church parking lot at one o'clock, I can do that," I told him.

He said, "Okey dokey."

At 1:00 p.m. the day of the picnic, I arrived at the church, parked my car, and waited. Even though it was a chilly day, the sun was shining. I got out of my car to breathe the fresh air and soak up the sun. As the trees swayed in the wind and I felt the brisk air brush against my body, I saw a white and blue Mustang GT zip along around the corner and stop suddenly to park. It was my date. We lovingly hugged each other, and I thought, *This one is different. He will accept me for me and not be all about my body.* With past boyfriends all they were interested in was my body. When we arrived at the park, he introduced me to his mother and other family members. One of the members of the church that we both knew from school was also there. He had been the principal of my high school and my date's guidance counselor. I overheard him say to my date and his family, "Invite me to the wedding." Two years later, he received his invite.

November 1984—Spirit Speaks to Me

In November of 1984, the man I had been dating for three months told me he loved me. I did not respond with an *I love you* in return for a few reasons. First, I just didn't know if I loved him yet. It was too soon. I had also just gotten out of a relationship before we met. Emotional attachments to my old boyfriend and his family were still there, especially his mom. We had liked each other very much. She had believed I was good for her son. Other past boyfriends' moms had also expressed this belief to me. It seemed to be a common thread.

So there I was, faced with the words *I love you* from my new boyfriend. I let him know I needed to tie up loose ends from a previous relationship. Even though this prior relationship was over, I felt I needed to go to his mom and tell her I wasn't coming back to her son because I had found a man who I believed loved me for me. I felt this was the right thing to do, so I did it.

The evening I saw and felt spirit speak to me was an absolutely gorgeous night. The sky was dark with many stars shining brightly. The evening was cool. My boyfriend and I were standing in a hallway, close to the door that led to the garage of my parents' home, where he had first said to me the words *I love you.* It happened at the end of our "together time." When I opened the door to let him out, never had I seen such a night. I walked out with him, viewing everything above me in the night sky.

For some reason on that night, I heard the night speak to me loud and clear. What I heard being said to me as I listened very carefully were the words, "This is the man you will bear children with. He is the right one for you now." That was a profound moment to hear the universe speak to me.

Was it spirits from the night sky? Was it God? I assumed yes, for I knew a God existed. I felt loved. I felt safe. It felt okay. Like I was all right, and I would oblige. It was as if a shooting star had come down and lit me up.

Knowing this, I was able to close one door and open another. There was a freedom that came from it. I was in so much of all of this feeling, knowing it and seeing it, that it inspired me to follow through with what I received from spirit from God. I trusted this man was the right man. I knew this information being given to me came from a higher place, a place where love resides, a place of light. I loved this beautiful light of the unknown heavenly places, this existence, helpers, guides, angels. All of it gave me a pleasant, comforting sensation. Now it was okay for me to move on to the next chapter of my life.

And so it began with this man I shall name Dominic, whom I would later marry. The interesting thing is that as we continued dating, I received another message but this time from an internal place. This one wasn't pleasant. It happened on a day when me and Dominic were walking around the neighborhood where he and his parents lived. We were walking hand in hand down the gravel road, talking about what we searched for in life. I didn't have too much to say because all I knew was that I loved him and wanted to spend the rest of my life with him. I knew I wanted children. I knew I wanted to stay at home to take care of my children like my mom had. It was important to me. I also thought of the idea of working part time after our kids were in school. We talked about this, and he said he was okay with that.

He talked to me about his older brothers; both of them were significantly older by thirteen and fourteen years. Both of his brothers had been married before and were now in their second marriages. As soon as he told me that both of his brothers had been divorced, spirit within me informed me we too would get a divorce.

This is hard to explain to someone who doesn't have the gift of sight. I was still new to this seeing, feeling, and knowing the unexplainable. These words/images/vibrations I receive come to me in an instant like a flash. It is like there is no space and time. It is a flash that comes to me so quickly; it is faster than anything you can imagine. It just is.

So I accepted the words I felt from within that I would be divorcing this man I was going to marry. I knew it would happen at some point in time, but I did not receive information about when or how it would come about.

There is a difference between me "seeing" premonitions and me "seeing," "feeling," "knowing" when spirit speaks to me. One comes from an internal guidance, my spirit within, my white light, and the other guidance comes from spirit(s) on another level. There is that outer source of spirit speaking to me and there is the internal spirit that speaks to me from within.

1984—Something Is Off

Dominic no longer had his blue and white mustang anymore. He had sold it and bought a brand new Ford Bronco. One day when he and I were together driving in his truck on Route 273, I noticed him glancing at a good-looking female runner. I noticed her too because I also saw how attractive she was. I wasn't jealous, but there was something in this moment between me and Dominic that felt uncomfortable.

There were also moments in our relationship when I was impatient with him. This bothered me about myself. My dad was also an impatient person. I knew he was intolerant of people performing tasks later than he expected, such as my mom not having dinner on the table precisely at 6:00 p.m. in the evening. It bothered me that I was like this myself. I knew this was something that would take me a long time to overcome. I knew impatience was something I would need to work on. I also got scared and anxious, worried that Dominic really didn't care about me. It seemed more like he was all about himself.

Dominic and I spent the next year dating. One chilly fall day, he sat me down to talk. He wanted to tell me about this job he got and about his plans for the future. He had been hired by a nuclear reactor plant that paid six dollars an hour. He explained to me the ladder he would climb in order to reach the position he sought. That was where the money was. He even explained to me how much he could make when he worked overtime, a double shift, a holiday, or even a weekend. Seriously, it looked good, and I was excited about this for me and for us. It helped me feel not so limited, knowing we would be able to go places and do things. It felt good to me as a twenty-year-old young woman, bringing me a sense that I would be taken care of and provided for.

A lot of young girls and women look for a Prince Charming to take them away, to take them away in so many ways. As for me, I just wanted it all: a good home, a secure family life, someone I could always count on. We looked like the perfect couple. Some would say we were attached at the hip. And we were. My father once gave me a birthday card that said, *The two of you fit together like peanut butter and jelly.* Now that's two peas in a pod!

I was afraid to be by myself. I was afraid to be alone. No one wants to be alone. Everyone wants someone to love them and to be able to give love to another person completely and freely. It is a human need and desire.

1985—Exciting Times

Being with Dominic was exciting. We loved. We laughed. Sex was good. We were young and free at twenty and twenty-four. We both enjoyed hiking, biking, working out, and driving along country roads, watching the scenery and looking at all of the styles of homes. We spent time dreaming together, enjoying the sun and the beach.

We shared many times together. Some we spent going to friends' weddings. One in particular was in Virginia. Both sets of our parents knew of this and trusted each of us in the care of the other. It was exciting for me to go away with my honey and meet different folks of an interesting mix. Dominic had kept up friendships with a few guys from his days in the U.S. Marines. One of these friends was the friend whose wedding we were going to support in Virginia.

I couldn't wait for the weekend to come so we could enjoy time together, doing what we wanted, having fun, dancing, and laughing at each other. Me being a shy, reserved girl who was afraid to dance, it took me forever to move my butt onto the dance floor at the reception, but when I went out, I went at it. I knew Dominic liked dancing, and I did too. I had gone to many dances in high school and at the Catholic church, but we had yet to dance together. When he did dance, it was hilarious. I laughed. I couldn't believe how bad he looked. It was embarrassing. I didn't even want to admit I knew him. I decided to do my own thing away from him. Now, looking back, it's more funny than embarrassing. Trips to visit with his friends were enjoyable because not only was I able to get away from my home life, but I was able to experience different areas of the East Coast such as Virginia, West Virginia, and North Carolina to name a few.

One thing I really admired about Dominic was how astute he was. And he didn't seem to be afraid to go off and do things. I saw how hard of a worker he was. While we were dating, he worked fixing boats. In the marines he fixed planes. I was amazed at how much he knew. His being a go-getter was an attraction for me.

At our one-year mark, he asked me to marry him. He made reservations at an upscale local restaurant. I was excited for this dinner date because I knew what was going to happen. I knew he was going to be giving me a ring and asking for my hand in marriage. After we walked into the restaurant and sat down to order, he looked like he had forgotten something and that he had something he wanted to say. I silently watched him, waiting for him to talk. He said something about his truck. I knew he thought he was surprising me with this ring, but he wasn't. It has always been hard for me to pretend I don't know things. My reactions reveal that I already knew what was going to happen.

After we enjoyed a most deliciously divine dinner, we got back into his black Ford truck, and he pulled out a small boxed gift. I open it, and it was a small, delicate engagement ring. He then asked me to marry him. I, of course, said yes. We decided our wedding day would be one year later on August 23, 1986.

1985—Getting Ready for the Wedding

As soon as I was engaged, I began making plans with my mom for a wedding dress and wedding invitations. Oh my gosh, I was so excited. I could not wait to start a new life with this man! To have someone by my side, loving me and caressing me, someone to snuggle with in bed at night or anytime we felt the need was a divine thought. My three sisters would be the bridesmaids and maid of honor. Since my younger sister and I were the closest, I chose her as my maid of honor.

As my mom and I searched for my dress, looking through so many books and patterns to find the right one, I had a vision in my mind of an all-white gown with a lace bodice, a sweetheart neckline, and cap sleeves. My mom still had her headpiece from when she wed my father in 1950, and she let me borrow it. She attached the headpiece to my three-quarter-length veil. In case you haven't figured it out yet, my mom made my wedding dress and the bridesmaids' dresses. My mom had sewn virtually all of our clothes growing up. That didn't stop when it came to my wedding gown.

1986—Day of Wedding

As our wedding day neared, I was excited yet frustrated that Dominic hadn't performed his responsibilities. Between my parents and him, he had agreed to post maps along the roads from church to reception. Both my mom and I were frustrated about his seeming lack of care. The maps were important for the guests who were not familiar with our town. It wasn't like Dominic didn't know how to perform missions. He had been in the marines for four years.

Many people were concerned about the reception because it was going to be outside in summer weather at my parents' home. But it ended up turning out perfectly. The day was gorgeous. Everyone couldn't believe the weather. For an August day to feel sunny and sweet with an actual breeze in the air was breathtaking. Angels must have been watching over us on our wedding day. My parents had rented two big tents for shade with picnic tables underneath for guests. Each table was decorated with carnations—my favorite flower—in pink, yellow, and blue. Most of the food was inside the house, and the guests were welcomed to serve themselves as they pleased. Our wedding cake was simple, three layers decorated with carnation flowers.

Dominic and I decided to wait until February of the following year to go to the Bahamas for our honeymoon. I had plenty of money saved to use for such an occasion. We enjoyed one week of sand and sun, away from the cold and snow in Maryland. It was a few weeks later that I miscarried.

CHAPTER 4

Children

1987—Miscarriage

My plan was to enjoy a few years of marriage before we considered having children. I had always known I wanted to be a mom. Children were a blessing and a gift from God that I wanted to benefit from. I even had the same set of goals as my older sister Lynette. She had waited a few years into her marriage before considering making the plans to extend her family. But that didn't happen with me and Dominic. Within the first year of our marriage I was pregnant. One spring day after Dominic left for work, I got myself ready to go to the gym. The gym I belonged to was an all-women's gym about thirty minutes away from home in a town called Elkton.

Where we lived, any place we went to took a while to reach. It was a small country-style community away from everything. There were plenty of trees and traveled roads that led to seemingly everywhere and nowhere at the same time. In my high school years, the kids teased students who lived in Rising Sun, using nicknames like rising scum. When kids have preconceived notions about the way other people and places are, it rubs off on others. So in my mind, I had never thought I would live in Rising Sun. However, once we settled there, I liked the area.

Dominic and I both loved the countryside. Before we moved in, when he was searching for a home, he had asked me to come along one day to take a look at one. He wanted my thoughts. As soon as I saw it, I loved it. I enjoyed being somewhat secluded. We had neighbors, but they weren't smack alongside of us. Close without being too close. We even had a yard all around us—front, back, and both sides. Behind our backyard was a corn field, so I enjoyed having this extra space. It was like a little piece of heaven. Different times of the year, deer would walk through our yard. I enjoyed seeing wildlife. They are beautiful animals. Living in Rising Sun, Maryland was close to Pennsylvania, so we often saw Amish travel through too.

I was driving along the road, ready and excited to work out. I was a little thing back then, no more than a buck ten. I had weighed and measured myself that day, just like every other day, so this day was no exception. *How could I gain an inch in my waist, hips, and breasts?* I thought it was odd. I had been hiding my eating disorder from my husband for a while. I wasn't going to say anything to him … yet. This gain of an inch here and an inch there was frustrating. I was obsessed with working out and watching what I ate. I enjoyed sweets, so I baked often. It gave me pleasure to bake for my husband and myself. I had learned many things from my mom; baking was one of them. My baking was a token of my love to my husband, putting sweets such as cookies, brownies, or cupcakes in his lunch bag. I was sure he got teased at work having wifey make him lunch, but this was me and one of my many ways of sharing love.

I arrived at the gym in my sky blue bike shorts and white sports bra with a T-shirt over top. This was a day I would never forget. I started my workout performing bicep curls, overhead presses, and tricep kickbacks using lightweight dumbbells, watching myself in the mirror. I remember it being warm and sunny that day, with barely no clouds in the sky. Me, myself, and I were enjoying ourselves, watching our reflection in the mirror, executing the moves. I couldn't understand why my breasts were bigger. Knowing my obsessive self, I wanted to do something about it and quick. I worked out harder and longer. I enjoyed looking good, keeping in shape, and caring about the health of my body.

I drove home satisfied with me and my workout. When I walked into my house and got to the top of the steps, I started having severe cramps. I figured they were menstrual cramps. I used to get them bad as a teenager.

In hopes of relieving my pain, I took pain pills. Four hours passed, and I was still hurting. I made sure to wait the advised four hours before taking additional pills. I did this for the rest of the day—three more times total, with the maximum number of pills allowed for an adult body. They were simply not working. The pain was the same, if not worse. Nothing I did helped. I took several more measures to ease the pain, such as lying flat on my back with heat, stretching, and prayer, to name a few. It was now nighttime, and I was ready for bed. There was still no relief. Among the pain, I eventually fell asleep while lying on my side and clutching my belly.

Awakening suddenly in the middle of the night with stabbing pain, I went into the bathroom to ease myself. There was blood dripping, and I suddenly heard and felt something drop out of me. As soon as it happened, I realized what it was. There was a mass of tissue lying in the toilet. I immediately went to my husband who was sound asleep in bed and waked him to tell him I had miscarried.

At first he just rubbed his eyes and said, "What?"

I told him, "Dominic, I miscarried."

He was in shock and didn't know what to do, so he called the only person he thought best to call—his mommy. Even though it was in the wee hours of the morning, she answered immediately. He informed her of what had happened, and she told us to get to the hospital immediately. Before we left, we wanted to take the tissue with us so we could present it to the doctor in order for him or her to determine exactly what it was. We wrapped the mass of tissue in aluminum foil, put it into a brown paper lunch bag, and handed it over to the doctors when we arrived. His mom wanted clarification that the tissue was in fact a miscarriage. I intuitively already knew this, but I knew this needed to be checked into, and I needed to be cared for. After the doctor examined me and the tissue, he said I'd had a spontaneous abortion. I did not like how he used those words, *spontaneous abortion*, because I would never abort a child. It wasn't something I believed in. I believed all children were meant to live no matter how a pregnancy happened.

I remember asking the doctor if he was able to determine the sex of the fetus. He said he was not able to do this because the embryo was only six weeks along. I hadn't even known I was pregnant until after the miscarriage. I wholeheartedly believe this child was a girl. I was informed by my doctor that if we wanted to get pregnant soon, we would need to wait three months. We waited, and three months later I was pregnant. This pregnancy was my oldest son. We had been married for less than a year at that time.

Each of my pregnancies was a joy. I loved the feeling of my babies growing inside of me, squirming, swimming, kicking, feeling life. My hopes were to have all of my births go as naturally as possible, even to go as far as water birth. Instead, none of them were.

My second child, born almost exactly two years later, was another son. Then twenty-one months later, out of the blue came my daughter. My vision from years ago had come to pass: two boys and a girl. When I was pregnant the first time around, I thought back to my vision, hoping the baby would be a girl. But it wasn't, and that was okay. When I was pregnant with my second child, I again remembered my vision, hoping it would be a girl, but again it wasn't. I knew I was going to have a girl, and I knew I was going to have three children, so when I became pregnant the third time around, I knew this time my girl was on her way. I also made a point to nurse all of my children.

1988—My Son Matthew

It was June of 1997, three months after my miscarriage, that I found out I was pregnant. We had waited the three months, per the doctor's orders, before we started to conceive again.

But before I tell you of my first son's birth, I want to preface it with an event I experienced with my closest cousin. As I was growing up, my cousin Dave often told me how I would make a wonderful mom, saying I would be a natural. It felt good to hear his words. Whenever Dave and I got together, we usually took walks just so we could get away from the grown-ups and have our own grown-up conversations. We talked about the stars and the moon and the beautiful sky. We talked about the girlfriend or boyfriend we had at the time. He'd tell me how easy it would be for any man to love me because I was such a sweet, beautiful girl.

Even though we were cousins, it was more like we were best friends. We saw each other maybe two or three times out of the year, so we made the best of the time allowed to us. I felt special in his presence. I think that back then, he helped me have more faith in myself. He helped me see some of the beauty within me, not just the outside physical appearance but the inner beauty of my spirit. That was what helped the most. So I would definitely say he was an integral part of my teenage years. When I found out I was pregnant, he was at the top of my list of people to inform. When I informed him of my pregnancy he was excited and proud of me.

Around two and a half months into the pregnancy, I felt flutters of a child inside my belly. Feeling the flutters turn to small kicks and then bigger, harder kicks was incredible. To feel the sensations of the baby moving around, poking his little foot or elbow what felt to be practically through my skin … wow and more wow. Why would any woman not want to experience the birth of her own flesh and blood? To me it was natural. Having this connection is similar to having a connection with our Creator. It is a feeling of eternity, of forever. We look to our Creator as a child looks up to his or her parents.

Matthew was born by C-section in March of 1988. His due date had been April 9. My doctor was concerned during my eighth month of pregnancy because my baby was in the breach position. He let me know that sometimes the baby would turn back around to a normal position in time for delivery. But at each checkup after the eighth month, the baby had not turned. My doctor ordered X-rays of my hips to determine the size of my pelvic bones. He informed me that even if the baby did turn around, my child wouldn't be able to pass through the canal because of the size of my hip bones and the circumference of his head. The risk was too high, so he scheduled a C-section. I accepted this, but I had been really looking forward to a natural birth.

One day when my husband wasn't working and we were waiting for my sister to come to visit us, I started to feel uncomfortable. I had back pain often during my pregnancy; this was due not only to Matthew being breach but also because of my uterus being tilted back. I took measures to comfort myself, lying flat on my back on the floor with a heating pad twice a day every day for a time. I often didn't know whether I was having contractions or not. This was my first child. I just didn't know. The Lamaze classes we went to helped, but once you're in the contractions, sometimes you don't know if your contracting or not. I thought I was, so I paid attention to the clock, timing the pain and paying attention to see if they got stronger, more intense, or lasted longer.

After an hour or so, we decided to go ahead and call my doctor. Hearing my husband talking on the phone with my doctor, I could tell the doctor wanted us to get to the hospital as soon as possible. As we were getting ourselves together, we heard a car pulling up our stone driveway. My younger sister and I had planned to meet that day for lunch.

As soon as she got to the door, I said to her, "Guess where we are going?"

"To the hospital?" she asked.

"Yes," I answered.

My sister was an X-ray technician who worked at the hospital I was going to, so she knew alternate ways to drive, and we ended up following her. She thought she knew a better route to travel that might be less stressful, with fewer bumps and turns. I don't think it helped much because I still remember feeling even the littlest of bumps, holding my belly, and doing my breathing. I was feeling and thinking, *Just get me there.*

When we arrived at the hospital, someone brought out a wheelchair, and they took me away, escorting me to a room. They strapped a belt around my big beautiful, no stretch-marked belly to listen to the baby's heartbeat. It seemed like so many people came and went to and from my room. It was frustrating but as each person came in I was told what would be done and why.

I was being prepped for surgery when the nurse told me my doctor was on his way. I had to be shaved where the doctor would make the incision. Another nurse who was attempting to give me an IV was hurting me. It must have been her first time on a real person. She kept jabbing and jabbing, not getting the needle in deep enough. Finally I told her to give me a break. When she left, I informed the personnel that I wanted someone else, someone who had been doing this for a while. Even then it hurt because I had been poked at so many times. The doctors expected I would be transferred to the operating room soon. Despite what seemed like a long wait, only a few minutes passed. I was later informed that I had to wait another two hours because an emergency C-section needed to be dealt with before mine. I was ready to get this over with. Finally, the time arrived for me to be sent to the operating room.

As I sat upright, hunched over, ready to have the needle inserted into my back to numb me, the anesthesiologist told me to be very still, not to move. I was as still as I could possibly be, breathing my lovely breaths. They numbed from the neck down.

My husband had to wait for me to be cut before he was allowed in to watch the birth. Before I was cut, a nurse tested my skin with a needle, pricking me from my leg up to my shoulder. She informed me to let her know when I felt the needle. She went so fast that when I said yes, she passed the mark. We did it again and again. She annoyed me. *That woman,* I thought. *Don't go so fast. How do you expect me to let you know the exact point if you are going to go so fast?*

As I lay there on the operating table, I asked, "Am I cut?"

They answered, "Yes, you are."

Okay, this was cool. I felt no pain. There was pulling and tugging, but I was fine. My firstborn son was born with his head up toward my breasts and his legs up the sides of his belly. He had lots of dark hair on his pretty little head.

"It's a boy!" they exclaimed.

I was ecstatic. I had always wanted a girl, but a boy is good too. When my husband held the baby up to my face, he looked so precious. Within minutes, I was out. Four hours later, I awoke in the recovery room.

My son Matthew had the sweetest smile, and his eyes were so slanted that he looked Chinese. Most hospital pictures taken of newborns aren't very good, but Matthew looked beautiful. With my breasts engorged, I had a very hard time getting Matt to latch on. I attempted many times with no luck. I was frustrated and worried that he wouldn't be able to feed on me. I wanted and needed this effort to be successful. I wasn't about to give up. The nurses were great in helping me adjust to the breast-feeding. We did many things to alleviate the condition, but nothing worked. I was so nervous because I thought I wouldn't be able to feed my child when I got home. I was determined to not bottle-feed. When I came home to spend time with my parents, Matthew took to me immediately. It seemed the problem had been tension. I remember holding him, settling him in my arms, and taking a deep, calming breath first before having him feed from me. From that point on, I never had trouble again.

I nursed Matthew for almost eleven months. I knew the importance of a mother's milk. Matthew started getting teeth at two months of age, and boy did it hurt when he bit me. After almost a year went by, it got to a point where it hurt so much that I had to consider weaning him away from my breast. I fed him one feeding from a bottle and the next from my breast until eventually they were all bottle and no breast. Matt was great. He slept like a champ too.

When Matthew was a little over two months old, I noticed that he looked different. I would sit him close to me and watch him as I lay on my living room floor, exercising. Lying on my side, supporting my head, and counting repetitions out loud, I looked at my beautiful son, who was sleeping sweetly. As I watched him sleep, I noticed that he appeared different. He seemed to have a different level of consciousness. I could tell something was off.

I immediately called our pediatrician and informed him of Matthew's odd behavior. He had also been throwing up everything he ate. I followed the doctor's orders and brought him in immediately to be checked. The description of my son's projectile vomiting and lethargy caused concern. The doctor felt around his belly, took his stats, listened to his heart, and so on. The doctor told me about a condition called *pyloric stenosis* and said Matt had it. He said it was common in firstborn males. It is a condition in which the valve of the pyloris has thickened, that allows food to move through the stomach and into the small intestine. The only solution was surgery.

So we scheduled the surgery. Matt would be in the hospital for only a couple of days. The hospital where the surgery was to take place was the same hospital where my younger sister worked and where Matt was born. She asked me who the surgeon was. I told her, and she was greatly relieved. She informed me that this man was not just an amazing surgeon but also a beautiful man who genuinely cared for his patients and was a man of great faith. I was blessed to know my son would be in such care.

I stayed at my mom's during this time because she lived closer to the hospital than I did. I was amazed at how late I could stay up when something happened to my child. I was with him at every moment. The surgery went well, and the surgeon wanted me to bring my son to his office for a follow-up visit six weeks later. If I needed to call him about anything prior to that, I was welcomed to do so. When the day came for me to take Matt for his follow-up visit, as I neared my destination, I soon saw that the doctor's office was a home office. He had a rustic-looking, professional home and a down-to-earth presence. This made me feel at home and safe. In those moments, I was glad for everything in my life.

Matthew did everything on time: turning over, rolling, sitting up, crawling, walking, and talking. He was pure joy through and through. Many times when playing outside in the spring and summer months, he walked barefoot in the grass to feel the earth beneath him. His father had a tractor that Matt loved playing nearby, pointing and squealing with delight. He loved playing outside. He loved reading. He would read for hours on end in his bedroom, sitting on the floor, looking at books one by one. There were many times when he was in the crib that he would reach over to where his Disney books were, and he would sneakily put his hand on them, look at me, watch me watching him, and then push the books over. Then he would laugh wickedly. Such a happy moment.

Sometimes when rocking him in the rocking chair or holding him as I swayed back and forth, lunging my legs side to side, I sang to him. This is a song I sang to Matthew as I sweetly and gently lulled him into a peaceful sleep:

> *I love Matthew, yes I do.*
> *I love Matthew, yes I do.*
> *He's the best baby in the world.*
> *I love Matthew, yes I do.*
> *I love Matthew, yes I do.*
> *He's the sweetest baby in the world.*

As each child came along, I used the appropriate name. I also sang nursery rhyme songs such as "Mary had a Little Lamb" and "The Itsy Bitsy

Spider." I loved how he loved listening to me sing and read him books. Each night at bedtime, I gave each child special attention by lying down with them in bed and reading them bedtime stories. I would also caress each one of them to sleep.

My son, my first-born son, is now a grown man with a wife of his own, working toward his own dreams. I instilled in him the ideal of never giving up on pursuing his dreams.

1990—My Son Jeff

In late March of 1990, I had a C-section while giving birth to Jeff. I had hoped to have a vaginal birth after my first C-section, but the doctors didn't want to risk it. I wasn't going to argue, so I trusted what they said. Besides, big heads run in the family on Dominic's side. As my belly increased in size, so did Jeff's kicks. A kick here and another kick there. I could see my baby's foot push into my skin. They always came as a surprise. I would be walking in a department store or a food store, and suddenly I would feel a kick or his hand stretch inside of me.

During this pregnancy, my younger sister and I were pregnant together. It was her first pregnancy. She was due after me, sometime in May. While I had a baby shower for her at my house, we wanted our mom to take pictures of us standing back-to-back and face-to-face. I had always known a day would come when we would be pregnant at the same time. Another of my visions had come to fruition.

On the day of my scheduled surgery, Dominic and I drove to the hospital to have the baby. When we got there, we of course needed to handle all the paperwork before they escorted me to the OB floor to be prepped for surgery. I was happy and anxious to see my baby, and I was sure he was anxious to see me. Dominic and I had never wanted to find out the sex of any of our children beforehand. I hoped for a girl, but if we were going to have a boy, that would be okay too. As long as the baby was healthy.

And that he was. Just like my first C-section, the anesthesiologist numbed me from the neck down. After being cut, I could feel the doctor pushing, pulling, and prodding around inside me to bring the baby out. Jeff was not a breech baby like my first, but he did have hair on his head. Jeff and I connected immediately too. It was a magical feeling, with sensations moving throughout my body and me seeing my baby's eyes and saying, "Hello there, sweet spirit. How are you? How is life?"

After my three-day stay in the hospital following Jeff's birth, I went to stay at my parents' house. After each child's birth, a week stay with my mom was a welcomed event. I took care of my child, and my mommy helped take care of me. I enjoyed this time with my mom before going home to my own house. I was so young and still fragile.

Jeff lost much of the hair he had over the next few months. I nursed him too but only for about five months. So many times when I nursed Jeff, my two-year-old son, Matt, would come around and say, "Put Reffrey down. Put Reffrey *down!*" Jeff would swing his head around to look at his older brother. Each time he did this when he was nursing, he pulled his mouth off of me … hard. Matt wanted all of my attention. Sometimes Matt would sit next to me and read his book, snuggling up close to my side while I nursed his baby brother. I could imagine how comfortable that must have felt for him as a child, nestled up next to his mom. Matt had another thing he loved to do to his younger brother. He had this fascination with Jeff's head, wanting to touch it, kiss it, sniff it, love it.

Life was pretty good. I felt blessed to be able to stay at home and have a husband that loved being a father. Dominic was a good dad. There were many times he helped take care of the children. We would take turns soothing them when they fussed or cried. When time came for me to stop nursing, he helped feed the children. When the children were sick, he helped clean them too. He did laundry, dishes, and cleaned the house. He was very good at cleaning. He got that from his mom and being in the marines.

My dear husband had two opposite sides that contradicted each other. Jeff was the son that would resemble his father the most… in looks and in his silly goofiness. Jeff adored the time at night when I caressed his head, face, and arms. This went on for many years, and this was the one thing he missed the most when me and his father separated. He also loved watching Bert and Ernie on *Sesame Street*. He even had the dolls, cuddling with them at night to fall asleep with while sucking on his two middle fingers.

Jeff turned twenty-one years old in 2011, embarking in his college studies of business management and athletic training.

1991—My Daughter Kelly

We found out I was pregnant the third time around when Jeff was a year old. I felt I wasn't ready to have another child so soon. I didn't know how I was going to handle three babies, a four-year-old and two in diapers. At the same time I also knew that this was to be my girl.

When I had my vision in college before meeting my husband, I had seen the three children that would come into my life. So with this pregnancy, I knew there was a reason to be pregnant. Even though I didn't *feel* ready, I had to be. This one was different. She never kicked. She would swim and swirl. I continued all of my activities of walking and exercising, just like I had with my previous pregnancies. With my precious bundle of joy inside of me, I was excited to be pregnant in the summer months so I could show off my baby belly.

Her due date was January 9, 1992. Doctors liked to schedule C-sections anywhere from seven to twelve days prior to the due date, so we scheduled surgery on December 30, 1991. On December 29, my husband and I—along with our two other children—were spending time at his parents' house. While there, I felt something move but didn't know what it was. I went to the bathroom and felt liquid dripping. I wondered if it was my water leaking. Since I'd had two C-sections, I didn't know what it felt like to a have my water break. My understanding of a water breaking was a huge gush of water pouring out of me.

I informed my husband and my mother-in-law about what had happened. My mother-in-law recommended I call my doctor. My husband called, and the doctor demanded, "Get to the hospital immediately."

So there we went again, on our way to the hospital. Once we arrived, they started preparation for surgery. A few hours later, little Miss Kelly was born with a full head of hair. She had so much hair that the doctors had a difficult time pulling her out. When I heard them saying they were going to use the vacuum to grab a hold of her head to help pull her out, in my mind I said to them telepathically, *No!* I just didn't like that idea. It wasn't proper. Human hands were better than a cold, metal object. Maybe this memory reminded me of when I came out of my mother's womb, the metal and coldness of objects.

Kelly got lucky and I got lucky because even the vacuum didn't work because of all her hair. To hear and see my baby girl was so precious, I couldn't help but cry. I finally had my girl. She was there. But for some odd reason that I couldn't understand, I didn't feel as connected to her as

I should have. *Why is this? This is the beginning journey of our lives together. I should be attached strongly with my baby girl like I was with my boys.* It took three to four months before my bond with her was strong. But once that happened, we were virtually inseparable.

Kelly loved the binky. She also was the one that nursed the least amount of time. I nursed her for two and half months. Since she was the baby, she was the one I spent the most one-on-one time with. The boys at least had each other to play with. Dominic was the last one to be loved and cared for. My babies were top priority. Many a night, I fell asleep holding Kelly, lying next to her, feeding her. My sweet, precious, darling daughter of many smiles had the biggest dark eyes and lots and lots of hair. We could never keep a barrette in her hair because it was so soft and slinky. It was no use to use a barrette in her hair because it always fell out.

I knew Kelly was going to be someone special and that somehow she would be helping me in my life. I didn't know how. I just knew she would. To this day, she remembers me telling her this. She was about two years old when I gave her this information.

One summer day in 1997 when Kelly was five years old, I was in the kitchen, preparing lunch for all of my family. Kelly came out of her bedroom, sat down on the floor in front of the closet door, and said, "Mommy?"

"Yes, Kelly?" I responded.

"Mommy, how will you need me when I get older? Why will you need me when I get older?" my beautiful little angel asked.

I could not believe she remembered me telling her that I would need her one day, that someday she would be helping me in my own growth as a person. She had been thinking about what I had told her. So much so that she had come out to ask me how it was that she was going to help.

I walked over to where she was sitting, knelt down to her level, and spoke to her. I told her, "Honey, I don't know how it is you will someday help me. I just know you will."

I don't think she cared for the answer because I wasn't able to give her solid information. Children are very smart and know so much more than we think they do. We think we know more than them because we're the ones who are older and wiser. While it is true that we know a lot about life as we live it, oftentimes we don't give children enough credit. When they are still very young, they are close to their spirits. They often can see and talk to spirits. They are their pretend friends. Our ghost friends. At such young ages, children are more able to listen, hear, and see what goes on around them much of the time. They are sponges, soaking up everything their senses are able to pull in.

When Kelly was a baby, she took the longest to fall asleep and stay asleep. We never had an issue with my first child sleeping. He always slept well and peacefully. When my second child came along, he didn't sleep as well as the first, but he still slept really well. When Kelly came along, she did not sleep as well as the second one. Not that any were bad sleepers. All actually slept well. It was just interesting to me as I noticed that with each child came a little more work with napping and sleeping. It seemed I always looked at the divine. How God, my Creator, prepared me for things, for life events, and for my overall picture in life. One step at a time. One event at a time.

The times I clearly remember are the times we were out on family visits. When we arrived home in the evenings, upon entering our house, Kelly would wake up. She would be wide awake and wanting to stay up for an hour or two. Of course, Mom and Dad were tired; we were ready for bed. One of us would hold and rock Kelly while the other parent carried the other two in from the car and carefully, lovingly laid them down in their beds. Kelly, I think she just liked staying up with us. She was more of a night person. To this day, she is still the last one to go to sleep. Our personalities as children stay the same into adulthood. It is the way we think, our beliefs, that can change.

Moments with Kelly were something all right. She hated doing homework, always putting it off until she *had* to do it. But one of the rules we had in our house was that homework came first before playtime. Well, maybe a snack and drink and then homework. So when I brought the kids home from school in the afternoons, Kelly was the one who threw a tantrum. She simply did not want to do her homework. She wanted to play. Anything but homework!

It wasn't that she wouldn't do her homework; she threw a tantrum simply because I, her mother, had the rule of doing homework before play.

Man oh man, she knew how to throw one too. Little Miss Drama Queen. Every single school day throughout all of elementary and middle school, she threw a fit. I thought it would never stop. I didn't know what to do about it. And even when she did sit down to do her homework, it took her forever. Two or three simple homework assignments carried on for hours because she would stop and play in between. As a parent, it was frustrating to say the least. She still is like this. Yet somehow she always seems to acquire good grades. There were occasions when she bullshitted tests and still did well. She's a pretty smart girl.

One of the other things Kelly would do upon occasion was bite. Oh my God, I never thought I would have a child that bit. I think she bit all of us at least once. Well, I am not sure about her father, but she did bite me and her brothers. I could never understand why or how she could get that angry.

Another thing I noticed about her—and this is not just a girl thing, though girls typically mature faster than boys—was that even at two years old she was emotionally mature for such a young age. She surprised and shocked me with some of the things that came out of her mouth, such as her emotional maturity when it came to relationships. An old soul within a young body—she says that now and has felt for years that she has an old soul.

At the time of this writing in 2011, she's nineteen. When she was younger, around twelve, she felt old then. She said to me a few times, "Mom, I am only twelve. I'm too young to have so many bones crack. I feel old." She doesn't see herself living a long life and doesn't plan on having children. I am okay with that. I just want her to be happy.

After all of these years that have gone by, my daughter has helped me simply by being her, speaking her mind, and telling me at times that I could be doing better as a mom. It hurt to hear that during my separation and divorce from her father, but at that time she was right about some of the things she said. I could have done better under the circumstances. During that time I had a tendency to talk to her about things I probably shouldn't have. It's amazing because she really did help in ways I am sure even she is not aware. It's like she helped me grow up.

By 1994, I had three small, well-behaved children, and all was good. They were dreams in my life.

CHAPTER 5

Marriage

1988—First Sign of Control and Manipulation

One summer day in 1988 when my eldest son was a few months old, my husband, Dominic, wasn't feeling 100 percent. It seemed like one of those twenty-four-hour viruses was going around. I belonged to the all-women's gym in a town called Elkton. That morning I had decided to go to the gym, which was around a thirty-minute drive from our home.

My husband was lying restfully in bed, all nestled and cozy under the covers, with medicine and water I had provided for him should he wake up and need it. I would only be gone for two to three hours. I came to him with baby in my left arm, hiked on my hip, let him know my plans, and gave him a kiss on the cheek. The words I heard come out of his mouth next surprised me.

He said, "If you leave and go to the gym, then you don't love me."

He had been with me when I signed up to be a member of this gym. He and I along with our son Matthew were together at this gym, when he had also informed me that he was fine if I wanted to get a job once all of our children were in school. We hadn't had all of our kids at that point, but we did know we wanted more than one. So that's where the statement came from. Therefore to him, love equaled me staying home, and not loving equaled me leaving to go to the gym. He also forbade me to allow Matt to be watched by anyone other than family.

The gym I belonged to was small. The babysitting room was in view of the weight and cardio areas. Whenever I went to the gym with my son, I always worked out in one of those areas so I could fully see him. Matthew was an amazing baby. He was so well mannered. All he did was eat, sleep, and play. He fussed only when he was hungry, when he needed a diaper changed, or when his teeth were coming through. I didn't think anyone could have asked for such a well-behaved child. My motherly instinct was also tuned in while I worked out. I could tell when he needed me, and I could tell the woman who worked as the daycare provider was excellent. I could see her love and passion for children. It helped that she had children of her own.

After my husband, the man-boy, said what he said, I protested slightly, telling him, "I won't be gone long. I'll be back in a couple of hours."

That didn't help. He again accused me of not loving him if I left to work out while he lay in bed sick. I showed him the water and pills I had brought him should he need them. He wasn't satisfied. He wanted me to stay home. I ended up choosing to stay home and worked out to an exercise video. Yes, he guilted me into it. I did it to keep the peace. The funny thing was that he slept for hours. He wouldn't have even noticed if I had left.

This was the first moment I can remember my husband putting control and manipulation into play. The following day when he went to work, I looked in the phone book for marriage counselors. There was a time when I considered pastoral marriage counseling too. Oh well, what a doozy, thinking that might work. I am not here to compare the abuse I suffered through from my father with the early manipulation from my husband. Each had their own demons. This was just the beginning of me noticing my husbands manipulative controlling ways.

Let me explain why I call him man-boy, if you haven't figured it out yet. I occasionally reference him as man-boy because even though he is a grown man, deep down inside he is still a little boy who wants a mom.

For example, when Matthew was a few months old, in the hospital for his pyloric stenosis surgery, Dominic and I were with him as much as possible. I was thankful that I was a stay-at-home mom and didn't have to worry about work relations. While Matthew stayed in the hospital, I pumped my breast milk to save for him to drink later. But Dominic became jealous of me nursing him. He felt he wasn't paid enough attention. Poor thing.

It was important for me to feed my child, and I felt if that was how I chose to feed my child, then my husband needed to deal with that. He needed to respect that. But he wanted to literally feed off of me like a baby too. I thought that was taking it a little too far. Since our first and second children were only two years apart, it didn't give Dominic much time in between to adjust to me taking care of two small children. Then when our third child came along, there was even less time in between. Boom, boom, boom—three children within four years. I often wondered how my mom did it with seven. She was a brave woman to have so many.

I had begun to notice the control and manipulation from my husband, Dominic, shortly after my first son was born. Interestingly, when I felt this control and manipulation coming from him, I began searching for a marriage counselor. I even made phone calls. Each therapist informed me that in order for him or her to see us, one of us needed to admit to an emotional disorder. *Well, that isn't going to happen*, I said in my mind. And I knew Dominic would never admit to anything like that. He didn't know how to admit his wrongs, all of his own issues that played into the breakdown of our marriage. I was not going to be the one to admit to such a thing in order to receive marriage counseling.

I don't remember too much between the first child and last child when it comes to my husband's domination and control. I think if anything, it happened subtly. Close to the time when Kelly was to turn three, something inside me snapped. I had no idea what it was, but I knew something had *hit* me, and I knew it had something to do with her age, with her turning three. I became quieter, more closed in. I had no desire to be with my husband. I did not have much desire to work on our marriage. There was too much going on with him attempting to control and manipulate my life, all parts of my life. I was tired of it. I was glad I had recognized this, and I wanted to know more about what it was about.

By this point I had become obsessive and compulsive with my exercising. Something had left me, or something internal had woken up, and the effect it had on my mind and body manifested negatively. On many occasions we talked about what we wanted to do with the house, inside and out. One of these things was to section off rooms in the basement. We planned that he and his father would work together to separate the area into rooms, putting up two-by-fours and paneling to make walls. Little actually got done; they only finished one room. It was decided we would use this room for business. It seemed that he and his father started projects but never complete them.

We also were involved in a marketing business in which Dominic would go full force and then slow way down. It went off and on for years. It was frustrating at times for me, but I supported him fully with the business. I believed he could do it and go all the way to be a leading millionaire, but it never happened.

When our divorce was finalized January of 2003, he remarried in March of 2003. This was when he decided to complete finishing our home. Everything we had talked about doing together, I saw him do when he remarried. New wife, new house upgrade. When we were together, he did nothing to make our house the way we dreamed. Instead, he spent money and time anywhere else but home, fixing other people's homes rather than his own. I was very angry that he did all the things with his new wife that he had said he wanted to do with me. I was angry and thought how ridiculous it was that he had gotten married again so soon after the divorce.

When we were married, Dominic did everything for his brothers and parents, leaving me and the kids—his family—less of a priority. Many years went by with a broken kitchen light and air conditioner. I am sure if you spoke to him today he would still be in denial over much of what he did or didn't do, but I know what I lived. My parents, sisters, brothers, and brother-in-laws saw and knew of things about which even I wasn't aware because Dominic had made comments to them about me.

Usually after a couple is separated, family members start speaking out about the other half. My family was no exception. This is when I found out Dominic had never supported me in my body-building competitions, which I participated in near the end of our marriage. During our separation, my mom later told me, "Hey, Barb, Dominic said to me on the day of your first competition that he wished you would fail so you wouldn't compete again."

He was intimidated by my muscles and my dedication to a sport that gave me joy and a sense of accomplishment. The bodybuilding competitions were my first real goal in my adult life. I not only succeeded, but I won trophies for them. My mom also explained to me that Dominic had made comments about how I was not being a proper wife to him because I refused to bear twelve children and I wasn't obliging his desire for several babies. I was shocked when she told me that. It opened my eyes and helped me see that he was even more controlling and manipulative than I had thought.

1995—My Unfaithfulness

When Kelly was close to turning three, something snapped inside of me, and I made a choice to do something I—at the time—felt I needed to do. My husband and I were not getting along at all. I kept feeling that he really didn't take what I had to say seriously and that I was one big joke to him. To him, I was there to have sex with and have twelve babies. I found out later that he really wanted a dozen kids. He wanted me, his wife, to be dumb, barefoot, and pregnant all the time.

We talked, I listened, and then he talked more. Our talks became fewer and fewer because each time I talked to him, there was a turnaround in the end and his way became *the* way. I quickly realized that my words meant nothing, so I figured why bother. He simply would not stop talking! On and on for hours sometimes he talked. It became sickening to hear his voice, hearing him eat me up or tear me to shreds as if I didn't know how to think for myself. If I didn't know an answer to his question, he became upset with me, claiming, "Yes, you do know the answer" or "What do you mean you don't know?"

Time would go by with me doing my domestic duties, pretending everything was okay, or I would just forget about it, let it go, leave it alone, etc., etc. Then I would start to feel good in my life and decide to open up to him again. I soon found myself right back where I had started, not being listened to and not being respected, and not just as his wife and the mother of his children but as a woman. It was like he was slowly taking away my womanhood and any individuality I had.

I was withering away to the dust, ready to be blown out the door. I was being brainwashed. There were times when he would not even allow me out of the house. On one occasion he decided to fix my car so it wouldn't start. I got ready to go to the gym, secured the children in the car, and started the engine only to find out it was dead. No sound, no nothing. I went to start the car again with no luck. *Oh shoot,* I thought and then said out loud to myself. I gathered the children and took them back inside the house, where I proceeded to put on one of my exercise tapes and work out.

When my husband came home from work that day, I informed him of what had happened. That's when he told me he had fixed the car because he didn't want me leaving the house to go to the gym. I was furious, but I held it inside. I knew well enough to not argue with him, knowing it would only make matters worse. I honestly don't know if this happened more than once or not. If it did, I didn't know about it.

After all three of the kids were born, his control and manipulation got worse. From 1995 on, everything continued in a downhill spiral. I became aware of the sexual abuse that had happened to me as a child when going through therapy, my anxiety rose causing me to binge and purge. I became more obsessive with weighing and measuring myself, exercising six to seven days a week. I also sought comfort in my passions and desires for the opposite sex. I was receiving no loving care from my husband. I felt trapped! I felt I had nowhere to go but into the arms of another man. I just wanted to be away from the man who hurt me and constantly blamed me for every single problem in our marriage. I felt ugly and no longer sexy.

After nursing three babies, I had lost my breasts. It took me over a year to decide to get breast augmentation. Dominic wasn't fond of it, but he ended up agreeing to the procedure. I was excited when the day came for surgery and pleased that Dominic stayed with me the entire time. He was with me when the surgeon came into the room to mark the areas where the implants would go. Naturally, in order to do this, the doctor needed to touch me. As soon as the doctor left, Dominic was all perturbed about him marking the areas necessary to perform surgery. I thought he was being ridiculous. I said to him in my mind, *Get over of yourself. Are you serious?*

Dominic was even abusive to me during sex. First, let me state that there are many forms of sexual abuse. When many people think of sexual abuse, they think it consists purely of a sexual encounter, of intercourse. But any time someone does something to you against your free will, it is abuse. Dominic looked at my parts like he was inspecting me like a doctor. It felt very invasive, so I would push him away. He accused me of not loving him, because if I really loved him, I wouldn't have a problem having sex with him.

So much was going on inside of me that I became very confused. I simply could not deal with everything at once. I was, however, smart enough to know that Dominic had his own issues to deal with and that he needed to stop casting blame on me. Over and over I heard from him, "If you didn't do this…" or "If you didn't do that, we wouldn't be in this place." Around the Christmas holidays, he commented to me that if we were ever homeless, it would be my fault, simply because of the fact that I had been unfaithful to him. He had so much anger.

You're insane! I wanted to yell at the top of my lungs. *You're the one that quit your job! You're the one that took early buyout! You're the one that cashed in on our retirement income! You're blaming me for your actions! Go to hell!* All of those thoughts ran through my mind. I could not believe this. Granted, I was no saint. I knew I had made my own mistakes along the way, but I had been humble enough to admit them to him. I admitted my eating disorder. I admitted I had been unfaithful.

There were many nights that I cried myself to sleep out of despair and confusion. I asked God for help, to guide me, to help me know what to do. I was involved with church and took classes to better understand and help myself. I had a small support system of friends with whom I hung out in a bible study group. The thing is, the closer I became with my Creator, the further my marriage deteriorated.

I asked God, "Why, God? Why is it that when I grow closer to you, I grow further away from my husband? Didn't you say marriages should stay together forever? Till death do us part?"

I knew something was not right. I knew I felt good feeling more connected to God, to spirit and to the spirit within me. It was even more important to me than anything in *the world*. As long as I stayed close to

God, my Creator, I knew that somehow everything would work out with me and my children. Through all of the abuse I *had* to keep my visions, my connection to God at the forefront of my mind.

1996-2001—More Abuse

When Dominic punched out the windshield of the car while we were driving down interstate 95, I was frightened for my life. I had been silent and remained silent. I was scared. I was scared he was going to stop the car and force me out, leaving me stranded to be raped and killed.

Moments before it happened, I had shared a dream of mine, expressing to him, "Wouldn't it be exciting to visit South Carolina? It is such a beautiful place."

He had gone off on me, accusing me that I wanted to go there because I had a boyfriend waiting for me. It seemed like every chance he got, he accused me of sleeping around with any Tom, Dick, or Harry. When he found out I had strayed, he had immediately thought I was doing anyone and everyone. Any male I talked to, he accused me of sleeping with. He accused me of sleeping with someone just because I had a business card that had a male's name on it. What a sick, sick man. In his mind, I was guilty of everything. It seemed he had me on trial in his mind all of the time.

My husband punched holes in walls and doors many times. The doors of our clothes closet and the bathroom closet door were damaged with holes. Once, as I sat on our bed, informing him that I would talk to my therapist about whatever I felt I needed to discuss, he threw a phone at me. Even though the phone didn't hit me, it passed my body and made a dent in the wall. He owned guns too and kept them in a safe place in the house, but I still had great concerns about his violent behavior. Sometimes I wondered if he was violent enough to carry out a murder. *Would he ever attempt such a thing on me?* I wondered. I certainly hoped he wouldn't.

I was too afraid at the time to do anything significant about all of this. I hid behind my fears. I played the victim for a while. I felt stupid, alone, and lonely. *No one really understands, do they?* When I met my best friend Barb, having her as a friend let me know that there was someone else out there whose situation was similar to my own. But in my own way, I still felt alone. I saw my friend Barbara as being more confident in who she was than I was. At least I thought this at that time. She didn't seem as scared as me. She voiced her mind to her husband. I didn't. I was afraid of conflict. (More about my friend Barb in a later chapter)

Another thing Dominic started to do when he found out I had been unfaithful was throw things at me, like a calculator or a phone or a hairbrush. I was never hit, but it sure scared the living daylights out of me. He often wanted to take all of my clothes and burn them. There was one instance when he specifically asked me to gather the clothes I had worn when I was unfaithful. I was so scared that I grabbed the clothes, handed them to him, and he forced me to watch them burn. Luckily for me, he didn't put me in the woodstove or hold my hand in the stove to burn me and yell, saying I would burn in hell for my sins.

The worst for me was when he used his controlling, believable voice to manipulate me into thinking I was the one responsible for everything wrong in our marriage. I started to believe that maybe I was the one who had a sex problem. Or maybe I was the one who wasn't thinking correctly about life, me, children, my mind, business, finances, etc., etc., etc. I could go on and on about so many times in my marriage when I thought I wasn't good enough or perfect enough or smart enough.

I knew some of it stemmed from my childhood, but not all of it. I knew, even if only a little, it was enough to help me save myself. I knew and believed I deserved better. I knew and believed that I deserved someone to love all of me and treat me the way I should be treated: as a gift. My visions gave me hope for a better future. I saw a better future. It just wasn't with him.

When I asked him if what he really wanted was me barefoot and pregnant all the time, he answered with an affirmative. He said, "Yes, that is what I want." And when he stood at the top of the stairs and told me he would never take the children away from me, I believed him. He swore on a stack of bibles. In lying to my face and to God, he didn't know what spiritual consequences there would be for him. I knew it wouldn't be good.

It wasn't until we were separated that I found out his main goal was to take the children away from me because of my unfaithfulness. Unfaithfulness is about the relationship between two adults. It has nothing to do with how a mother cares for a child. This goes to show what a person will attempt to do in the face of raging anger. After our separation, many people expressed to me that they felt he had been brainwashing me.

My Womanhood

In my marriage, I hid my voice. I became scared to voice how I really felt for fear of not being accepted as a whole woman. At the time, I did not know how to be a whole woman. I was under the belief that a man was supposed to take care of me and be my sole provider and that women ruled under men. Yet, at the same time, I also felt and knew intuitively that I was powerful and worthy of being treated with honor.

I continued to live out of fear because I had grown up that way. How was I supposed to just stop that fear? I had all of these dreams and desires, and I had visions inside of me that I could see unfold. Even as I knew divorce would come to our marriage, never would I have guessed it would happen the way it did. I saw visions, pieces of my future, but I didn't see the details of how these visions would take place. I didn't see how the divorce would unfold. We're not supposed to know everything. Just enough.

I had visions during my marriage that I knew would happen after the marriage was over and dissolved. With each of these events, I wondered, *How is that going to happen?* This other man that I saw in one of my visions would enter my life. This man seemed to be a partner in life. The vision I felt I could tell was a vision that would come about years later. I could see that we were a team. I could feel that he needed me more than I needed him, but we still helped each other. I knew and could only go with the information that was given to me. So I remained faithful and true to this information from spirit. Was it a vision, some might wonder? Or were spirits showing me pictures of my future life?

When we start thinking the worst, we have the potential for the worse to happen. I could have told Dominic, "You made me cheat." But I didn't do that. I knew I was the one who had willingly made that choice. Dominic, the man-boy, made his own choices. Whether he could admit to them or not is another story.

These visions, premonitions, even prophecy some might call it, were what gave me hope. They pushed me through the difficult times that came forward in my life. Never did I think I would live through such abusive, controlling behavior from my husband. It was subtle in the beginning. Little comments or looks here in there. With each child, the subtle comments became less subtle. I felt like I had nowhere to go and no one to turn to. I did not want to tell my parents anything about it. I had no real friends until I met Barb. It was just me, husband, and kids, so I hid it. Many times I think I just didn't pay attention to much of it in the beginning. I let it burrow down inside of me.

We were married for nine years when it got out of control. It was his way or no way. What he said and what he did were two completely different things. He claimed that he wanted me, his wife, to be an independent thinker, to have my own thoughts and ideas, and for me to express them. But each time I expressed myself, he always turned things around, making it look like his way was ultimately the better way. I think he enjoyed using the Bible on me too, that how we as women, wives, must be submissive to our husbands. How the husband is the head of the household. I thought, *Yeah right. Not like this.* I found out much later during my teachings from my Angel Bearer of Light that the spiritual leader of a household is the woman.

Women are to be cherished and honored. We are the nurturers and caretakers of children. Our intuitive emotional makeup is stronger and more powerful. We are more connected to our Creator because we too create life. It is because women have life-giving force within our wombs. Only women have this. I have given birth to three beautiful children, two boys and one girl—exactly what I knew and saw. I saw and knew I would be going through a divorce. The spirit did not give me the details of how it would all come about, just that it would happen and that there would be a purpose to all of it. I had such hatred for men, yet at the same time I loved men. How is that? There was a reason, and I'm so glad for everything because I know there is a spiritual reason for everything.

2001—Spirit Speaks Again

After Dominic and I separated, when we had our first court order, we were ordered to undergo a psychiatric evaluation to help determine outcome of our children's placement. The court also ordered us to go through mediation at a Family Services facility for the pick-up and drop-off of the children.

My husband filed at the courthouse first, so he was the plaintiff and me the defendant. I remember despising that because I was the one who had been abused. I felt it was unfair and wrong for me to have to come through the back door. As time went on, I learned that I wasn't the only woman to have to come through this door. Because of this, I was given the opportunity to really see what it is like for the men.

There was one event that happened while I was sitting in the waiting area of the family services facility to pick up my children that I remember. We were just newly separated while going through mediation. Mediation lasted for quite some time while we were going to court for child custody. Spirit spoke that I, Barbara Anne, would be helping men. When I heard this, I thought, *Yeah right. How in the world is this going to happen? I hate men right now. They are all pigs, ignorant and immature.* But I listened and kept this in the memory bank of my mind.

I also wondered, *how would it be that everything spirit spoke would come to fruition?* Visions I had seemed so distant yet also close from me in that moment; however, I still kept them close to my heart. Even though some of these visions were far and some were close, I believed. For instance, seeing myself as a personal trainer was a close vision. Seeing me owning my home was a distant vision. I had dreams like you too, such as a new car. My visions were my dreams.

These visions/dreams come from a higher place. Some may say their visions come from their higher selves, from spirits, from God, from their guides. It doesn't matter where you think they come from. What matters is that you believe and work toward them, trusting and surrendering all along the way. It's like being implanted with an information chip, and this information holds people, circumstances, and evidence of what you can have. It shows you what is waiting for you as long as you hold the divine close to you, be grateful, and remain thankful for all that you have right now. It is important for us to surrender and keep our faith. You hold within you all the powers that many great beings, such as Jesus Christ, held.

I have learned from my Angel Bearer of Light that we must follow through with any guidance given to us from higher powers. We must trust this guidance. Not only do we have the choice to follow these inner promptings, but we have the choice to not to. If we choose to not follow, we have only ourselves to blame and no one else. If we willingly choose to follow through with our inner promptings, our spirit, and our gut instinct, then we can rest assured that it is always for the good, that somehow, in some way, we will be blessed. It may be in the form of a physical blessing such as money, or it may be the pleasure of being blessed with a smile from a stranger or a neighbor who has never smiled at you before.

This world in which we live, this small planet called Earth, is all very small compared to all the other planets in our galaxy and other galaxies. But the spirit world is everywhere all of the time. It is all-knowing, all-encompassing, and all-amazingly huge. It is so big that there is no way we can comprehend its vastness. Infinity is forever. Can you see forever? Can you *see* forever?

CHAPTER 6

My Therapy

When I was going through therapy in 1995—the beginning of many years of therapy, some good and some not so good—I persevered through it. I first ask you to forgive me as I write the following. It's not so much a blur as it is a lack of awareness of the timing of events because I felt I was tossed around like a bowling ball. I lost track of who, when, where, and what I said to each therapist. At points during the years between 1995 and 2002, I saw many professionals—from psychologists to psychiatrists and social workers—and they were all good in their own rights.

If my husband didn't like one for whatever reason, he took me to someone else. Desperation was part of it, I'm sure. I believe the first one we went to was a female psychologist at a hospital in the Baltimore area. She wanted me to tell her what it felt like to be with someone else. I answered even though I didn't think it was an appropriate question. I wasn't sure what to do, so I gave my answer. My husband and I both agreed we did not like this particular therapist.

Upon leaving the hospital, when I went to sit in the backseat of the car, my husband stopped me and said, "Sit up front." It was a pleasant surprise. Somehow we managed to get through a weekend retreat we had planned. When we returned home, we searched for help. He found a psychologist in Pennsylvania. I remember it was a long drive to get there. The psychologist talked with my husband alone for an hour, and then he talked with me. Originally, my time with him was meant to be for one hour, but it turned into two.

The psychologist asked me, "How long have you been married?"

I said, "Nine years."

He was quite surprised that we had made it that long. The doctor continued, asking me questions such as, "Have you ever been sexually abused?"

I sat in my chair, looking at him, and thought for a moment. A few thoughts went through my mind: *We have been talking for a long time now, and I can see he's not an idiot. He makes a lot of sense. Was I abused?* We are sitting face-to-face, and I said to the doctor very openly and clearly, "I don't know. Not that I can remember."

He invited my husband to come back into the room with us for a final note. One of the things the doctor informed my husband was the following: "What your wife needs is a sense of her own independence. I recommend for her to take some college courses and have a part-time job. She needs to have something for herself."

Oh my, Dominic hated hearing those words. He wasn't going to stand for that, someone telling him his wife needed a job and college courses. He certainly hadn't heard what he expected the doctor to tell him about me. I am sure Dominic wanted the doctor to tell him how wrong I was or how bad I was, wanting him to fix me. That was the first and last time we saw that doctor.

It was interesting that in the beginning years Dominic had told me that when the kids were all in school I had his permission to seek part-time employment or schooling, but now with the psychologist recommending me to do it for a sense of independence, he was against the idea.

1995—Psych Ward

So it was off to a new doctor that Dominic had searched for. I had no voice in the matter. He made the choices. This time it was another male doctor. He was worse in my eyes. He had no clue who I was or what I had gone through. There was virtually no communication between me and the psychiatrist. All he wanted to do was figure out what label to attach to me. I was a number that rolled through his psych ward.

This all came about Monday morning when I walked into the gym I belonged to at the time. It was summer. I was itching with life-giving force, and I couldn't stand being in my home anymore. I hated my husband with a passion. He hurt me, pushed me, and abused me in every way but physically, so I had left for the weekend. When I entered the gym that morning, I went into the restroom and saw one of my friends. I was anxious, wanting to talk to her. I told her I was scared of my husband.

Cops arrived at the gym and waited for me to come out of the restroom. I wondered why. I hadn't done anything wrong. I had escaped the home I was living in, wanting to be left alone. I found out later that my husband had manipulated my parents to signing an agreement with him to have me escorted to a psychiatric hospital. Of course I was scared. I didn't know what was happening. The friend from whom I was seeking advice and support thought it best I go with the cops. I really wasn't so sure about that. But I went anyway.

The local hospital was right around the corner, so it didn't take very long to get there. I was extremely upset, angry, and agitated that I really didn't know what to do other than remain quiet. I was not in the mood to talk with anyone. No one knew what was going on behind closed doors. I found out later that Dominic had hired a private investigator to follow me. I also found out that he had manipulated my parents into thinking I was going to harm myself, which of course was not the case. I simply wanted to be in a safe place away from my husband. I hadn't known how to do that. Running away was the only option I felt I had at my disposal at the time.

When I was in the local hospital, my parents, two of my sisters, and a friend were called. They all came to the hospital to see me. My younger sister told me that she thought it best that I go ahead and admit myself to the psychiatric hospital because she thought Dominic would take the children away from me for good if I did not. I felt I had no choice. The nurses and doctors who thoroughly evaluated me at this hospital let me and everyone know that they had no cause for concern. They didn't believe I would hurt myself or anyone else. I remember the nurse telling me that I had the free will to sign the paper or not. But upon hearing my sister's words, I was scared that Dominic would truly take the children away from me, so I signed it.

The next thing we knew, the staff did their work and prepared an ambulance to escort me to a psychiatric hospital in Pennsylvania. I spent four long days there. This was where I met the psychiatrist who really had no clue about what I was going through. I thought about my children a lot. I wondered where they were and what they were thinking and how much were they missing their mommy, for I was definitely missing all of them greatly.

My husband, man-boy, had manipulated me. If I hadn't obliged to his request, he would have taken the children away from me forever. All because I didn't love him anymore and had found someone else who loved me for me. I was infuriated at him. I cried for myself. I cried for my children, my children who needed their mother. They were only four, six, and eight at the time. I knew there was no reason for me to be where I was. We needed marriage counseling. I needed help with the sexual abuse I had been traumatized with. I needed help with my eating disorder.

I went from this hospital to a group center for outpatient services. In there I requested to see a therapist who dealt with sexual abuse survivors. She confirmed that it was highly probable that I had been sexually abused as a child. I was thankful for her professional opinion. I was now starting to get somewhere.

Once I completed my final duties at this facility, I wanted to find a therapist who specifically dealt with eating disorders and sexual abuse trauma. I found her through the phone book. I let my spirit rule me in that moment. When I made the phone call and we talked, I felt very comfortable with her and extremely at ease knowing her expertise was in both of those areas. Until she told me, I hadn't known that 75 percent of women who have eating disorders have at some point in their lives been afflicted with sexual abuse. I was fascinated. She helped me like no other therapist ever has.

During some of our meetings, we had couple's sessions. My therapist had asked Dominic if he was willing to see her partner for individual sessions. He agreed. He had only seen men before. Now he was open to seeing a female therapist. He went to her for a period of time and then quit. I continued to stay on for as long as necessary. I knew I was important enough for myself and my children.

Before he quit, after Dominic had been seeing his own therapist for a while, my therapist and his therapist thought it was time to have a couple's session again. My therapist made an observation to Dominic. Very careful with her words, she said he was needy. My husband hated the word *needy*. Yes! Finally, someone other than me agreed about his sensitivities and neediness. It had been ridiculous. I could not stand how needy he was. Dominic did not want to hear this, of course.

When the hospital had transferred notes about me to her, they had made me look like a lost case. Her response to me about this was, "You are definitely not the worst case at all." What she saw in me was a hurt woman who suffered from post-traumatic stress disorder. She had easily put the pieces together. That's what you find when you have a true professional taking time with a person and not treating his or her patient like a number. My dear, lovely therapist, Wendy, also received a four-page, front-and-back, letter from Dominic on what he thought was wrong with me and gave her suggestions for ways he thought she should fix me. She never read that letter from him, only ripped it apart and threw it away. It was all nonsense, and it was not her job to focus on him. Her job was to focus on me. I was her patient, not Dominic's. She wanted to hear what I had to say in my own words, not to be colored by his. More great relief. It had been forever since anyone thought I was worthy enough to be listened to.

1995—Revelation

In 1995, our children were three, five, and seven. I had been going through a lot and felt scared and alone. This was the day I had seen my first counselor. It was evening, and I fell fast asleep. I awoke suddenly upon receiving a deep, profound knowing. Woken by a higher spirit, a nonphysical being, an angel—I don't know what it was, but it was profound. I received the following message: "Yes, you were sexually abused as a child."

Things were now starting to make sense. During the day while my husband was home, I walked outside behind our house in the cornfield to blow off steam. I ran, I cried, I screamed, I called out to my Creator, ran some more, and cried some more. I stood, arms raised to the sky, looking into the sky, and said out loud to my Creator, "I will do what you have called me to do for the rest of my life. I give my life to you."

I was so determined to be the vessel of light my higher God had called me to be, in whatever fashion was so fit for me to be. I asked for protection and guidance. Soon thereafter came individual therapy for me, individual therapy for Dominic, and couple's marriage counseling. I had been tossed around like a bowling ball from one therapist to another because Dominic didn't like any of them. I felt I really had no choice or say in the matter. This was a rough road that only pushed me further away from him. But it is interesting how it brought me closer to God, my Creator—the one who means the most to me. I followed spirit, not man. Yes, I made mistakes along the way, but my search was always for truth, for higher knowing.

1998—Refusing Me To Go To My Parents' at Christmas

I thanked God, but it was tough for me to learn and grow while living in the conditions I was in. There were good days, and there were bad days. One year, one of the really bad days was when Dominic did not allow me to spend Christmas with my family. The only reason he didn't want me to go was because he thought someone else might show up. That someone else was my sister's husband. Granted, I didn't particularly like my brother-in-law either, but I saw no reason for that to stop us from spending Christmas day with my family.

My mom was very sad when I told her Dominic wouldn't allow me to come over. Later in the evening, after my family left my Mom's house, my cousin called. He wanted to spend time with me. Because of how far away we lived from each other, we weren't able to see each other often. My husband gave me permission to visit. Remember my cousin Dave who I mentioned earlier? That was who called me. I eagerly got myself together and left, anticipating a talk. It was breathtakingly refreshing to get out of the house, see my family, and talk freely with my cousin.

1999—Telling My Mom about the Abuse

In 1999 I was working at the local Mission Center and also had a part-time job cleaning houses. I was still married at this time, and it was during this time that I was competing in amateur bodybuilding competitions. I thought cleaning houses would be an easy way to make money to help out in paying for my training and the products required to compete.

I met many people and made good friends at the gym I belonged to. I made friends with one girl in particular. As we talked, she mentioned she was looking for someone to hire to clean her house. I told her I was cleaning houses on the side and looking for prospective clients. We exchanged numbers and met the following week. When we met, I wore a sweatshirt saying something about answered prayers. She noticed this and proceeded to let me know about the church she attended. She went on to tell me about an all-women's event coming up and asked if I would be interested in going with her. I accepted her offer. I remember the lady I saw at this women's event was an author, and I was intrigued by that, for I too knew that I would one day write a book.

As I began a new journey with this friend and now a new church, I increasingly received more mental memories and bodily memories of the sexual abuse that had happened to me as a child. One of the houses I cleaned happened to be my own parents' home. My dad was still alive at this point, and I had been cleaning for my parents for a few months when the following memory surfaced.

My parents own a colonial home that is more than 4000 square feet. I had cleaned much of the house and was now headed into my father's bedroom and bathroom. The bedroom itself wasn't so bad, but on this particular day as I cleaned the shower in the bathroom, I had an intense memory that shook me to the core. My memory was this: While in the shower with my father at such a young age, he picked me up in his arms rubbing my little body up and down his private area, belly and chest so he could feel me against him. I was also forced to give him oral. It was sickening for me as a child to have to go through the whole ordeal. After the memory it was extremely difficult to finish the job of cleaning my parents home. I knew in that moment that I had definitely been abused by my father. This day was also the day I knew I could not and would not be able to clean my parents' home again.

Since my mom had me clean her home once a month, I had time to work with myself on how to tell her why I would not be able to clean her home anymore. It took a lot of strength and courage for me to face my mom with this news. I knew I wanted to talk to her face-to-face and not by phone. It was the proper thing to do.

I reached out to her by phone shortly before my next scheduled cleaning. I asked her if she could please come over because I had something important to talk to her about. She gladly accepted. When she arrived, I knew it was going to be difficult for me to tell her and for her to hear, but I had to do this for my own health. We sat down and ate lunch before I opened my mouth and told her the following: "Mom, I need to talk to you. The reason I asked you over is because I cannot clean your house anymore."

I told her about a bodily memory I'd had, not going into details, but I told her I had been sexually abused between the ages of three and five. I went on to say that the abuser was a member of the family. She was in shock. She wanted to believe that she would've noticed something like that when she bathed me. She said something to the extent of being around me 24-7. I didn't say anything, but I thought, *Mom, it would be impossible for you to be with me 24-7. You had seven children to take care of.* I also didn't know if she realized that sexual abuse didn't necessarily mean sexual intercourse.

Another day while visiting my parents' house with my husband and children, I had an anxiety attack that stemmed from the abuse. All I remember is that something hit my core, affecting me on such a level that I felt a threat to my being as a whole. I went and found my husband to tell him we had to leave and leave right then. I informed him to immediately pack up the children so we could go. I went upstairs to the bathroom to gather my composure in order to keep from leaving in a dramatic way. I decided it would be a good idea to talk to my mom before we left.

I found my mom, told her I needed to talk to her, and asked if we could go outside. Of course she said yes. As we sat on the front porch, I told her how determined I was to cut the cord in order to not pass down family issues to my children, that I would be the one to stop this. She understood what I meant. As I watched Dominic with our children outside, I felt good and proud of myself for telling my mom such news. We then left.

CHAPTER 7

Meeting My Best Friend

One day in 1999, I asked my Creator—no, I pleaded with my Creator—"Is there anyone out there like me in the same situation?" Each day as I drove the kids to school, I would pass a Mission Center, and every single day for a year their business sign called me. It caught my eye, or better said, my eye caught the sign.

One day I realized that I had better listen to myself and stop by. I knew time was running out. This door would not be open for me much longer. I knew the opportunity was now. On the way back from dropping the kids off at school, I stopped by the center to check it out. I decided I would volunteer my time in the food shelter. As soon as I walked in, I asked the first person I saw who was in charge. The person I spoke to happened to be the director of the center. We sat down and talked. He told me everything I needed to know about the shelter, but he also gave me information about a part-time paid position. I was ecstatic. I liked that even better. Work part time three days a week, maybe four hours each day, for $60 a week. I remember thinking Dominic would be okay with it because 1) it was a "Christian organization" and 2) it would be during school hours. The director asked me if I wanted to come back the following day and meet the girl I would be working with. I said, "Yes, I would be happy to stop by."

I had recently had a dream about a girl. She had blonde hair past her shoulders, wore jeans, and was skinny. After I dropped the children off at school the following day, I stopped by the center. The director invited me in and introduced me to the girl I would be working with. Her name was also Barbara. I was fascinated by her in that we shared the same first name. When we started working together, we talked about our children and husbands. Conversation about kids started easily. We found out that each of us had three. We both had two boys and a girl, and our children were around the same age. The only difference was that her girl was the firstborn, and my girl had been born last. What's even wilder is that both of our daughters had the same name, and our boys had the same first initials. It was wild with all our similarities.

As we started to feel more comfortable with each other, we continued talking and mentioned our husbands. We found out that we both were going through a lot of the same conditions with our husbands—control, manipulation, verbal abuse—and we both had suffered sexual abuse as children. I told her about my prayer, and she told me that she had prayed the same thing. There we were, the answers to each other's prayers. We now had a safe friend and confidant to go to. I expressed to her my dream of seeing her just as I saw her then. She was a bit surprised that I had seen her in my dream as she truly was. We stayed friends for many years. She was there for support on the day I separated from my husband. Meeting her and having our friendship was a saving grace for me at the time.

Never devalue the gift of such a good friend if you are so blessed to have one!

CHAPTER 8

Hard Times

2000—Bodybuilding Competition

In 2000, I was still working at the Mission Center as an intake officer, and my friendship with Barbara had blossomed. We were always there for each other, loving and supporting one another. We were each other's stronghold.

This was also the year I decided I wanted to physically transform my body by taking a body transformation challenge. In order to track my progress, I needed to have before-and-after pictures taken. I also needed to record a start weight, my body fat, and my inch measurements, and I needed to use the products this particular company sold. I let my fingers do the walking in the yellow pages, looking for nearby gyms and calling them to see if they measured body fat percentages. I found one in Aberdeen, Maryland, that met my needs.

The next day while the children were in school, I decided I wanted to do this and get the transformation started. I drove over to the club and went inside, where I met a gracious young lady and asked her, "Who do I talk to about getting my body fat taken?" I heard her call out a man's name. He was a personal trainer there. As he came around the corner, I noticed he was a very attractive man. He introduced himself as Nick. My thoughts ran wild because he was so handsome. I could tell he took care of himself. I told him about the challenge I was doing, which he was familiar with, and we went downstairs so he could document my weight and body fat.

I remember stepping on the scale with all of my clothes on. He was not able to find his calipers, so I did not get my body fat measured on that particular day. We scheduled another day to measure my body fat. Even though I knew my husband wouldn't care for me becoming a member of this gym because it was co-ed and I hadn't consulted with him first, I signed up anyway. I was guided internally. I trusted myself.

The following school day after dropping off the kids, I went in to work out. Nick took me aside and asked if I had ever thought about competing. When he asked that, a memory of a vision passed before my eyes. I knew my answer would be yes. But I told him I would think it over for a couple days.

I waited, letting the two days pass. Then at that point I said to Nick, "I will do the bodybuilding competition, but only if you train me."

"Of course," he responded. That was his job.

He informed me of the cost for ten sessions. It was a bit much for my budget. Nick believed in me and decided to go out of his way to pay for my sessions out of his pocket. We came to an agreement that I would pay him back in increments as I could. He saw my potential and trusted his own instincts.

The body building competition I entered was held in Baltimore, Maryland, in July of 2000. Training started three months out. Nick started me on a diet and had me eating no more than seventy-five grams of carbohydrates per day. My start weight was 124 pounds at five feet and two inches. I had put on almost twenty pounds of muscle and fat during the past three years when I started adding more weight resistance. Now I was ready to lose some of the body fat along with leaning out. I lost weight quickly, losing a pound a day for eight days, maintaining this loss of weight throughout training until a few days prior to my competition day. Three days prior to a competition are what is called "dry out time." To "dry out" means to deplete the body of excess water in order to visibly see more clearer muscle definition on the day of competition.

In bodybuilding competitions, a competitor can enter several categories. In this competition, I entered myself in two: lightweight and masters. A masters division was for women thirty-five and over. One of the things I had to do to prepare for my competition was practice moves. Some of these moves were for my abs. I had a very difficult time doing these abdominal poses in front of a mirror, not just because they were more difficult poses but because it brought forth sad feelings about my sexual abuse. I would walk through my bedroom and pass by the mirror, not wanting to look at myself, even in as good of shape as I was in. All I wanted to do was cry. I fought against this urge and did my abdominal poses anyway. I knew the importance of getting through this in order to compete.

My trainer wanted me to practice every single day, sometimes several times a day to get the moves down. I listened to him. The diet and exercises I did were much easier than practicing poses. This was something I wanted, and I wanted it badly, so I did everything in my power to get myself where I knew I wanted to be.

As the day of the competition neared, I was excited and nervous at the same time. Not only did I have to perform poses in front of a crowd, but I also had to come up with my own one-minute routine. I would perform my routine onstage in a bikini. The song I used for my routine was called "Brick House." Remember that one? Believe me, I was definitely nervous, but boy did I end up having fun. At the very end of my routine, I closed it with one of my famous splits. I ended up winning first and second place. I was very happy with my results since it had been my first show. It was the first goal I'd had in my adult life. I did it, and I succeeded. I won. It was an amazing journey to watch my body transform the way it did.

During the time of my competition, I had also been seeing a therapist who was helping me with the domestic violence situation I was in. I went to the shelter in my local area. The only way I was able to make my counseling sessions was by telling my husband that I was seeing her for the sexual abuse that had been perpetrated by my father. He had no clue that I was seeing my therapist because of him.

From her I found out more and more about just how controlling Dominic was. I even went so far to ask her a certain question to which I honestly did not know the answer. She informed me, "If you say no and he does not respect your answer by doing that behavior to you anyway, then yes, Barbara, it is abuse." I was flabbergasted. To find out my husband had been abusing me in every way but physical was an interesting realization.

After my first bodybuilding competition, I signed up for another one. It was scheduled for October of 2000. Again I set my goal and succeeded. I signed up for another, which was set for April of 2001. Little did I know at the time that my husband, man-boy, had been tampering with my mail. I wondered why I hadn't heard from the national office of the bodybuilding federation concerning the April competition. I made a phone call and found out they had not received my information. It was then that I became suspicious that Dominic was tampering with my mail. He had done it before.

When I went to the gym the next day, I asked the gym owners if they would allow me to fax my paperwork to the bodybuilding federation. They said they were okay with that. So now all was well. At least that was what I thought.

2001—Time Leading up to Separation

I had started seeing my therapist at the domestic violence shelter in April of 2000. I was allowed under law to receive this help for free for one year. April of 2001 arrived, and my competition was nearing, as was the end of my therapy. The competition was set for end of April. My birthday was April 19. Interestingly, at my first competition my number had been four, and in my second competition, my number had been nineteen. Now, with my third coming upon me, I wondered what my number would be. Would it be twenty-six? Would it be sixty-five? These numbers are all very significant to me because they represent important dates in my life. April is not only the fourth month, but also my birthday month, nineteen is my birthday day, the twenty sixth was my best friend Barb's birthday and also the day I was to compete, sixty-five well that's just another significant number I choose to not disclose to you, so I wondered: *Would twenty six be my competition number? Would sixty-five be my competition number?* I just wanted the days to go by so I could compete.

By then, living conditions with my husband had become unbearable. I was living with so much pain inside. My solace was my competitions and being amongst friends at the gym, my home away from home. That and, of course, my children. It was hard sometimes to contain myself and put on a front. The children knew a lot. They picked up on everything. Children are sponges picking up on so much information. It is important to listen to them and yes, sometimes even heed their advice. At such young ages they are smarter and wiser than us adults at times, especially when they recognize how one parent treats another.

Several times my children asked me, "Mommy, why don't you and daddy get a divorce?" My worst fear was that as they grew older and started to become independent in their own skin, Dominic would use his control and manipulations on them. I found out later as we went through our separation and divorce and in the years that followed, he did just that. It tore me up inside to hear from my children some of the things he did and said to them, sucking their minds dry of any independent thinking. Thank goodness that to some degree all three of the children recognized this pattern, but at the same time, they had a hard time seeing it as a control issue.

The weeks prior to April 26 were scary. I had much anxiety, always wondering what he was up to. My husband, man-boy, had been acting weirdly lately, looking around for something. Intuitively I knew something fishy was going on in those weeks.

Somehow I found out that he was lying to me, misleading me into thinking he was going to work every day, but in actuality, he was not. He was out doing things, planning something. I could tell he was planning something, and it didn't feel good. Not at all. At this point I was still going through my own therapy, but my year was going to be ending soon. *Then what will I do?* I asked myself. Other than the one weekend I ran away, I had left a few times, but I just couldn't bear to stay away. I was too scared. I had three precious children that I loved. I think I would've left very easily if I had been working full time with a career. I would have just packed my bags and the kids' bags and gotten the hell out.

During therapy, therapists often suggest for their clients to journal. It's an easy way for patients to vent feelings in a safe manner to be discussed later in therapy if they so choose. Writing my feelings and thoughts down was a safe way for me to vent everything that was going on inside of me. I journaled everything: daily life events, dreams and goals, dreams I had at night, my feelings toward my man-boy husband. I remember my therapist telling me not to be afraid to say whatever was going on in my thoughts and mind. So I did just that.

These precious journals that I so cherished with all my heart were stolen by my husband. April 26, 2001 was the most horrific day of my life. Yet at the same time it was also the most freeing.

April 26th, 2001—Day of Separation

April 26, 2001 was a school day, and I dropped the children off as I headed over to the gym to work out, tan, spend some time in the sauna, and practice my bodybuilding moves for the upcoming competition. My birthday had just passed, and I thought it very odd that my husband never said happy birthday and didn't give me a gift or a card. It was the first time in all our years together that had happened.

When I went back to school to pick the children up, I didn't see them anywhere, so I went to find the aftercare teacher and asked her, "Where are the children?" She informed me that Dominic had come in earlier that day and picked them up.

"Didn't you know?" she asked.

"No, I did not," I answered her.

I was frightened to say the least. I was not sure what to think or do. I was both scared to go home and scared not to. I decided to go see my best friend, Barbara, and talk to her so I could manage to calm down before heading home. It helped, but I was still scared. I didn't know what he was capable of. My thoughts went to the worst-case scenario. I knew he wouldn't hurt the children, but I was greatly concerned for their psyches. My worst fear was that he would take the children and leave the state.

When I got home, I was relieved to find that he and the children were there. After going to the domestic violence shelter and seeing my therapist for a year, one thing I did know was that I was not going to play pretend anymore. I decided it was time I speak up so I could find out what had happened earlier that day in school.

When I entered the house, I had a conversation with my husband that didn't go over very well. I had asked him why he took the children out of school earlier that day. He refused to answer. I asked again imploring to know why. As he stands a foot taller hovering over me he sternly says to my face, "I'm not talking to you!" This in turn scared me more. He walks away going into the childrens' room looking out of the window as if he has a plan. There I was, standing up for the first time to the man who had been dominating my life for almost fifteen years, and I was being ignored and talked down to again. He continues his plot of walking away and ignoring me that I now have become enraged. I say calmly but loudly, "I am their mother. I have a right to know where you took the children today. I will not be silent anymore. Where did you take my children?!" As he continues to ignore my pleas for answers I follow him into the dining room.

An altercation took place, with me turning to firmly grab hold of his arm. I, at this time, was also wondering why he would be wearing a long-sleeved shirt on such a hot day. *Was this part of his plan?* I thought. I *knew* something was up. He was doing weird things, acting oddly, differently, not his typical Dominic. It was not necessary in his work to wear a uniform. He could wear what he wanted as long as he looked professional. I had seen weird patterns of behavior from him the past two weeks. I could feel and sense that something wasn't right. He had been looking all over the house for something it seemed he could not find. I had wondered and said to him, "What are you looking for?" He didn't say anything. He was extra quiet, which was totally not normal for him. He typically would talk my ears off so much it made me sick to my stomach. Besides, my keen, intuitive spiritual eye was seeing loud vibrations of hurt coming my way. I have never been wrong when it comes to my gift of sight, seeing the seemingly unexplainable.

Before I knew what was happening, I heard him on the phone with 911, and I caught the drift of the conversations between him and the person on the line. I heard him making me out to be someone I was not. I heard Dominic telling the operator, "No, she has no weapon. She is just standing there." I stand silently for a moment wondering what is going on. I am numb with everything and nothing, not knowing what to think. I couldn't believe what I was hearing. I used this moment to tell him I will fight for the children. "I will not allow you to take the children from me." He will not win this battle. It is now my turn to fight back....legally.

The children are in the living room playing video games. I wonder. *Can the children hear? Can they hear anything their father is saying?* I tremble inside. Dominic says to the 911 operator, "She is standing by the dresser five feet from me." Moments later, the cops arrived to question our domestic altercation. We each gave our story of what happened. I admitted that I had grabbed my husband's arm. That was enough for the cops to make an arrest, handcuffing me, informing me of my rights to remain silent. I was a simple, sweet, honest woman, so I spoke the truth. The county cop I spoke to was very nice to me, and I could tell he could see what was *really* going on. There were holes in walls and the doors of our bedroom. Doors that had been torn down. However, because of the way words were written in the law, he ended up having to arrest me. It was a great shame that it came to such an end, especially with the children there. This was worse than anything I had endured. It was very humiliating. There was one thing the cop said to me that I will never forget. He said, "One step at a time." I kept that in my memory and repeated his words many times throughout the remainder of my life.

The separation and divorce process was an ugly battle. When I spoke with the judge later that evening, he asked me if I had someone to call to stay with. I thought smart and informed him, "Yes, I do. You can call the domestic violence shelter. I have been going there for treatment for a year." He made a phone call, and I was escorted to the shelter immediately. My escort just so happened to be the same county cop who had arrested me. I was happy it was him.

The bright sun woke me the following morning, and I made phone calls to my mom, my lawyer brother, and my personal trainer to let him know I wouldn't be making my competition. My brother found me a very good lawyer that dealt with domestic situations. He also commented to me, "Another brother-in-law I don't like." As soon as I was able, I followed through with the steps my brother suggested. I was a stay at mom and had no place to go so my mom being the beautiful and wonderful mother she was, gladly accepted me back into her home for as long as necessary for me to get myself on my feet. She also helped me out financially in order to pay for the lawyer.

I spent the next five years with my parents and attended more therapy at the domestic violence center. I continued not only with one-on-one therapy but also group therapy. I was so relieved to be out of the situation I had been in. Even though it was the most horrific day of my life, it was also the most freeing. I felt for my children, but I knew he would not harm them physically. I, at the time, knew myself well enough. I knew I wasn't psychologically capable of taking care of them for the time being. I needed help!

It was time now for me to be free. I looked forward to seeing my therapist. My enlightenment was important and crucial to me to succeed in this life. This may have been easier said than done; but it takes a lot of work to learn to become free and enlightened. Time was a crucial part of the process. I wanted and needed to start this whole process of working toward my enlightenment. My first step was gaining full-time employment. As a stay-at-home mom taking care of my family for almost fifteen years, I had lost touch with the world. I needed to become more powerful within my own self in order to help myself and my children, even if I was only to make eight dollars an hour.

The divorce was a long ugly two year battle over custody of the children. It wasn't final until January of 2003. Shortly after, in March of 2003, my husband remarried. It's funny how he and his new wife never had children. All he had wanted was for me to be barefoot and pregnant. She didn't even know what it was like to give birth, for she had no children of her own.

2005—Standing up to My Dad

On that day of April 26, 2001, after meeting with my therapist, I called my mom to come pick me up. As I said earlier, I stayed at my parents' home for five years. In 2005 during my stay, there was a fire in the house.

I awoke in the middle of the night to what I thought was a clock alarm going off, only to find out it was the fire alarm. It took me a while to wake up and realize that was what it was. I got out of bed, walked over to my mom's room, and woke her up. We immediately went downstairs and saw fire coming out of the trash can in my dad's computer room. It had set the drapes ablaze. My mom quickly put it out with water and a fire extinguisher. We opened some windows to help disperse the smoke from the house.

My mom yelled and screamed about my father for smoking his damn cigarettes and throwing the cigarette butts in a trash can that had paper in it. I found out that this was not the first time it had happened. I was scared and didn't know what to think. I went upstairs to wake my father, only to find he was already awake, fully aware of what was going on, yet he sat there and did nothing. That angered me even more.

Shortly later, I heard my parents arguing, yelling, and cursing at each other downstairs in the kitchen. I heard my father yelling at my mom, saying that he would continue to smoke cigarettes and that he could smoke them any damn time he wanted to. To me, he had absolutely no care at all for anyone other than himself. Standing upstairs at the top of the steps, listening to their words reminded me of a time when I was twelve years old, afraid and quiet. I was an adult now, and I told myself I would not stand there and be quiet, saying nothing and doing nothing. It was time for me to stand up to my own father.

I went downstairs to where my parents were, and I said with determination and anger to my father, "You don't even care if you kill your own family?"

He waltzed himself past me back upstairs, yelling on his way. "I'll go smoke a damn cigarette now if I want to!" And that was precisely what he did.

The very next day I packed my bags and moved out to stay at my younger sister's house for a while. That lasted until I got a phone call from my mom telling me my dad said he was sorry, that he missed me, and that he wanted me to come back home. I wasn't too sure about it, but I ended up going back. Honestly, it was getting to be too much living at my sister's house. She had a husband and children of her own to take care of. I couldn't seem to get away from domestic abuse. My sister was living her own.

Learning Lessons

Life certainly is a lot about learning lessons. There were times I doubted, feared, or felt insufficient. I had to go through these lessons for myself. As my Angel Bearer of Light informs me, "Mistakes are for learning from, never to condemn."

I am now in my mid-40s, having lived with anxiety surrounding me in my childhood, in my marriage, in the loss of a job, in finding work in order to make money I needed to pay bills. There were many tough moments, and as I look back now, I find that I am amazed at myself. I am amazed that I remained strong enough to get through those times, strong enough to not give up, strong enough to continue believing in me and in where I knew I needed to go. I still had many dreams I wanted to bring forth. I can tell you all sorts of things to be and how to see, but what we need is the how. How do I love me? How do I have patience? How do I have peace and joy all the time?

It is possible, and it is a lot closer than you realize. Just like everything in life, it takes consistency in doing and rethinking how we behave, how we think, how we act and react to people and life circumstances. To look beyond ourselves, we first need to want this so badly that we are willing to go beyond. We need to not give up on ourselves. We need to not give ourselves excuses, saying that we don't have enough time or that we want a partner in our lives first and then we'll do it. Typically we humans have this thing inside us that makes us do things backward. We think backward. It's not just negative thought that gets in the way but the backward way of thought that has come to us from many different places such as society, church, religion, and our own parents. In my opinion, we have been brainwashed.

In my own life I have noticed that if I would just think the opposite of what I felt like I wanted to do and then do it, I would be a lot happier and thinking and acting from a loving state. So much of what we say or don't say and what we do or don't do is the opposite of what we really need to be doing and saying. For instance, back in 2008, I came across a man who was telling me about certain books. He called them "the green books." These books were written from an ascended master through a man. As I read the first two books—which were written in purple ink, by the way—I could feel the vibration coming from their words and into my being.

Every single night I took the time to read, and every night my body felt and held on to so much heat energy. I heeded what those books said and applied it in my life. The first week I did this, my income doubled. I was simply amazed. I thought, *Wow this works!* I had been living day by day, never knowing if I was going to make enough money to pay my bills. Acting this way created anxiety. When I received a client, relief came. As long as I was making money, all other parts of my life felt better. It was like I was using money as a means of happiness, even though I knew it was not money that makes a person happy. I was smart enough to know that happiness comes from within, not from anything external. I needed to learn to let go and let be.

My first conscious memory of living in anxiety was when I was in middle school. I was fearful every day when my father drove up the driveway, not knowing what mood he would be in. I didn't even know what the word *anxiety* meant or that I was living with anxiety until I went into therapy many years later. I just knew I was living in fear.

Later in life when I was going through therapy at around thirty years of age my therapist asked me, "When you were younger, did you feel like you were walking on eggshells?"

I understood that, and I answered, "Yes, all of the time. For as long as I can remember."

As my marriage crumbled, my husband's manipulation and control became worse. My anxiety rose as the months and years went by. In my many attempts to leave my husband, I froze and couldn't do it. I didn't want to leave my kids. At the time, I felt that if I left, I would have to leave my children behind, and I could not and would not do that. I loved them too much. I wanted to love my children as much as I possibly could and in the best way I knew how, each day and in each moment.

And just like when I was a child with anxiety, wondering what mood my dad would be in when he got home, I was also anxious when my husband came home from work. This happened near the end of our marriage. I never knew how conversations would go. Many times there was no communication unless we absolutely had to talk. There were times when I would communicate with him, only to find out during conversation that it was all about him and how he thought things should go. My words never had meaning. They had no value; therefore, I felt I had no value.

After going through our talks so many times, I decided that enough was enough, and I stopped communicating with my husband completely. The marriage was over. We may have been living together, married, but there was no marriage left to salvage. April 26, 2001, was my last day of living in the same house with my husband. It was a day of horror, but at the same time it was a day of freedom because I was away from him physically. I had traveled a tough road, and the road ahead wasn't looking very easy for me either, but it was going to be better than what I had just gotten out of. I knew at some point, somehow, and in some way, I would make it on my own. I also knew I wasn't going to barely make it on my own. I was going to be successful on my own … without help from a man.

CHAPTER 9

A New Beginning—Dreams, Desires, Goals

2001—Looking for a Job

I immediately started looking for a job after our separation. As a stay-at-home mom with only a high school diploma, I had no clue how to write a resume. So I got help with that. I found out through the local community college that an organization would help me for free. I went and received help in putting one together. After completing the final resume, I made several copies and sent them off to potential employers. I put in many miles of footwork, traveling to gyms and physical therapy offices all over the area.

Within one month I had a job at a physical therapist's office right down the street from my parents' house, not more than ten minutes away. When they called me, we set an interview for the following week; the start date was scheduled for the week after that, full-time with benefits. Having this job allowed me the flexibility to go to personal training school. After completing personal training school, I continued working at the physical therapy office and worked with personal training clients in their homes.

Having my certification also allowed me to teach senior fitness classes. One of the teachers in my personal training school called me to ask if I was interested in a job teaching exercise classes at a senior center. I had never been interested in working with seniors, but I thought I'd give it a shot. So I accepted his proposal. The job involved teaching fitness classes for seniors in the surrounding area five days a week. I went in for an interview and was hired immediately. Over the course of years, my students and I grew very fond of each other, so it was a sad day when I decided it was time to leave. Everyone wished me the best, and we hugged and kissed our goodbyes. Everything I did was but a steppingstone that helped me see what I ultimately wanted, and that was to be a self-employed, successful business woman helping others grow physically, mentally, emotionally, and spiritually.

Shortly after separating from Dominic, in June of 2001, I got out a piece of paper and wrote down all of my dreams. I highly suggest you do this for yourself. Here are mine. I present them to you now:

- Become a personal trainer
- Become a certified nutritional consultant
- Make twenty dollars an hour
- Purchase an SUV with cash
- Make fifty thousand dollars a year
- Work in the TV field
- Own my own home
- Purchase a new vehicle
- Hire an interior designer when I move into my house
- Pay someone to clean my house

Read on and see with your eyes, hear with your ears, listen with your heart what I have to express to you when it comes to all your goals, dreams, and desires. Each and every one of mine was a new beginning for me toward an increasingly prosperous, bountiful life. The rest of this book will concentrate on my life moving forward and share some of the lessons and truth teachings I have learned from my Angel Bearer of Light along the way.

Goals, Dreams, and Desires

Goals, dreams, desires—we all have them. What do you dream? What do you desire? What are your goals professionally, personally, spiritually, and socially? Which are most important to you right now in this given moment? How deeply do you dream? How big do you see? Are you the type of person who reaches high, or do you tend to settle for less than what you know you can have? I always say to dream big. You might just get it. So why not shoot for the stars? You will never know until you go for them!

I've always been one to dream big, and I honestly don't care what anyone else thinks. It's my life. They're my dreams. You don't have to like it or think, *Well, that's not reality, Barb.* The negative thoughts you think or the negative things people may say to you should mean nothing to you because our Creator placed inside of you, placed inside of everyone, a breathing, thinking mind. This power we all have allows us to have the power to dream the dreams we dream. All a goal is and should be is a dream set into action. It always has been that way for me. In the difficult times and in the beautiful times, don't allow your dreams to float away in the ocean or drift fleetingly with the wind. You are a child of the great Creator of life. The great mystery is in the mystery. It is fun to have mystery. We don't need to know everything all the time.

"If you can't stand the heat, get out of the kitchen," is an old saying, a saying I don't agree with. I suppose it depends on the subject matter; for example, if it really is hot, then yeah, get out. Sometimes this saying is said to a loved one in different terms: "If you don't agree with me, get out." It is my understanding that this is an unproductive way to go.

"If you can't stand the heat, get out of the kitchen" is not the way to treat your man or woman. To be a real man, to be a real woman, we must stand up for what we want. It is time we have a serious and honest talk with ourselves about our wants, needs, and desires. It is time to love ourselves unconditionally, to care enough about ourselves that we cast no judgment upon ourselves or others for their dreams. No dream is a dream if there is an intention to hurt another, whether it be a friend, a foe, a nationality, or a country.

Be real with you. Be real with your partner. Being real with yourself means not sacrificing your own divinity. This is about you, the divine being you are, not the selfish physical you. In order to figure out where you are coming from, you may need to back up and step out of the situation for a bit. Take some deep breaths. Go for a walk or a run, clean your house, refresh, allow yourself to get away, and ask yourself, "What is it that I want? What is it that I need? What are my true longings?" These are not selfish acts. These are divine acts. Being true to you. You cannot be true to others if you are not true to yourself first. Everything will always start and end with you. Sacrificing yourself, such as staying in a marriage for the kids, is not healthy no matter how *good* it looks on the outside. Staying in a marriage for this or for that, staying in any relationship for unnatural reasons is unhealthy.

In my marriage, I didn't realize some of the decisions I made were coming from an unnatural state of being. I know more now, which is why I am writing this book to tell you my story. I am writing to help you make choices from the divine. In order for you to make choices from the divine, you first need to recognize that you have a divine source within you. I give these events from my life to you to help you see what the divine looks and feels like, what it is like to know *you*. I believe that in telling you some of my life events, I will help you get a better picture of the divine within you so you can learn to see, feel, and know yourself.

I love you, and it is my desire for you to meet yourself, to get a grasp on the real you behind the flesh of the body that carries you around, to better understand your mind, your sight, your hearing, and all of your senses. Those senses are here to help you. Allow the white light in you to guide you, to coach you. You are your own healer. You are love. This creation, this white light that resides in you. No one but your own self can take away anything from you. So don't do it. Love yourself enough to be who you really are, because you are always worth it. And I will tell you again, *you are always worth it*. Everyone around you and in your life feels this part of you when you let it shine. Don't ever hide your light. Hiding your light casts shadows on others and yourself. Do you want your shadows casting a storm over the people in your life? Your loved ones?

I think this is why we seem to hurt the ones we are with. We hurt the ones we love most. To stay true to your dreams and desires, you must stay true to the divine in you. But how do I find me, you might be asking, if I don't even know who I am? How do I find me if I don't know where to begin? What you do is ask you. Ask the divine being that resides within you. I suggest that you go look at yourself in the mirror. Look straight into your own eyes and ask, "Who are you? Who am I? What do you want from me?" Then say, "Speak to me. I am listening." Then believe. Just be open to being aware. Then go about your day-to-day activities.

Back in the day, when I was still married and going through my first bodybuilding competitions, I remember feeling and knowing I wanted to become a personal trainer. I *knew* this would be a way for me to help people. It was a purpose, a desire, and yes, a dream. I have always known I wanted to be part of the health field, to be able to truly help someone in such a way, to transform their bodies and lives. My desires were in the right place. My reasons for wanting to do this were in the right place. I felt good inside whenever I thought about it. So go with what feels good to you on the inside. That's where the divine lies. When things, people, and desires feel good to you on this deeper level, this is a sign you are in the right place.

As I was getting ready for my competition, practicing my moves, posing in front of the mirror, eating the foods my trainer told me to eat, doing the exercises he prescribed, I had in the back of my mind this desire of becoming a personal trainer. Interestingly, back then I also felt really deep inside of me that there would come a time when I would be writing a book based on my life events. I saw this vision and knew it would someday happen, but I often wondered how and when.

One particular day when I was in my bedroom, practicing bodybuilding moves, my husband and I were talking. I opened up to tell him my dream of becoming a personal trainer. I told him I believed I could help save people. I remember him laughing it off, proclaiming, "You're not going to save people through personal training. No one is going to come to you to hear about God."

He didn't get it. He didn't understand. In becoming a personal trainer, it wasn't my intention to save people through the word of God. I wasn't going to just start preaching the Bible as I was training them. If someone brought up the subject, I would express my thoughts and then leave it up to the other person.

My husband continued, "You'd be better off and you could save millions of people through..." He mentioned a money marketing group. I really didn't care so much for that. Even if I only saved one person through my work, it would all be worth it. Besides, I loved watching my body transform and knew I could help others transform their bodies.

After my husband and I separated and I was living with my parents, I went to personal training school. I am proud to say I did this on my own with no financial help from other people. I was on a path to one of my dreams. It is one of the best decisions I have ever made because it lead me to more dreams I wanted and knew I would receive. I stayed close to my heart. I always had hope, faith, and love, allowing my visions to guide me forward.

Let's get on with more of the dreams I wrote down. You already know I separated from my husband on April 26, 2001. You know that in June of 2001 I decided to write down everything I wanted to have in my life. I dreamed big and wrote down things I would achieve, no matter how big or far off they appeared to be. I even wrote down the type of man I desired.

When I wrote down my goal to make fifty thousand dollars a year or even twenty dollars an hour, it was huge considering I was making only eight dollars an hour at the time. Like I said earlier, dream big. It doesn't matter what others think. These are your innermost desires, and they are there for a reason. They were placed inside you for you to serve and be fruitful. When you feel these burning desires within you, I am telling you there is a way! You are the one who has to decide to tap into it. Once you make the first step, the next one will show itself and then the next, and then the next, and then the next! Know you. Love you. Be you. Have fun dreaming.

2002—Making Twenty Dollars an Hour

When I became a certified personal trainer/certified nutritional consultant, I began making twenty dollars an hour. I achieved it by becoming a subcontractor with a local gym. Twenty dollars an hour was my cut from them. I also had a part-time job teaching fitness classes to seniors at a local senior center. I received twenty dollars per class I taught. As part of that job, I traveled to different locations in the surrounding area, teaching fitness classes for seniors.

During this time, my boss with the senior center asked if I wanted to be part of a televised exercise show for the city of Wilmington. I eagerly and excitedly said yes. It was a chair sequence, healthy lifestyle exercises for those who were not as mobile as others. I also worked for a company located in California, performing health checkups around the state of Delaware. This also paid twenty dollars an hour. At one point I had four part-time jobs at once, and I enjoyed every one of them.

2004—My SUV

I dreamed for an SUV. My reasoning for wanting an SUV was because I planned on using it to travel from one place to another in my personal training. I needed the room for transporting equipment.

One day, my son, Jeff, and I were looking around the Internet for vehicles. This took time, as I am particular in my wants. My son found a Hyundai Santa Fe he thought looked nice, so he had me read about it. It sounded perfect. When I had written down the SUV on my dream list, I had also written down what I wanted inside of it. I knew I wanted leather seats, automatic windows, a CD player, tinted windows, decent gas mileage, two to four years old, a price I could pay in cash, and an obviously safe vehicle. Everything I read in the description fit.

I drove up to the dealership the following business day to test drive it. The salesman found a Hyundai I liked, so we took it for a ride. I ended up loving it. The salesman commented that it was out of my price range for all cash but that I could get a loan to pay the remainder. We worked with the numbers, and I said yes. I felt somewhat uncomfortable, but I said yes anyway. As I sat on it for a couple of days, the uncomfortable feeling didn't go away. I decided it wasn't the right timing for me. I knew I had three business days to make a final decision to back out, so I did.

A few months later, on New Year's Eve, I was looking on the Internet, searching for the website of the dealership where I had test driven the Hyundai. Low and behold, the vehicle was still there. I immediately called my salesman, not caring that it was New Year's Eve. I wanted to make sure I was going to be the one to snap up this deal. He followed up with a call the next business day. It was in fact the exact same vehicle.

I drove up on a Tuesday, went through all the paperwork, and came home with a new vehicle, paid for in cash. Well, it was new to me, even though it was two years old. That's new enough to have a new vehicle. And the price had gone down by three thousand dollars. I will take this event one step further and tell you that as I was going into my savings account to verify with the dealership that I had the money, I just so happened to remember the account number. That was amazing, as I usually didn't go into that account.

2005—Making Fifty Thousand a Year in the TV Field

In 2005, I was preparing for my first figure competition. I was currently working as a personal trainer for seniors, training in a gym, and traveling to clients' homes. While I was in my competing mode, people typically noticed me. I knew a lot of people, and a lot of people knew me. One of these individuals owned his own business. He approached me, asking if I knew of anyone who knew how to work in front of the camera. At first I said I wasn't sure, but then I thought for a moment and a girl came to mind. I suggested this individual to him. Shortly afterward, I realized that I had been in front of a camera when I did an exercise show for the seniors in Wilmington. Even though I did not have much experience, I was willing to learn. We talked more, and he keenly intrigued me with his idea, so we traded business cards.

The next day, as I was traveling the roads, going from one place to the next to teach my seniors, I received a phone call from this individual. He asked me if I was interested in the proposal he'd made, and I said yes. He informed me more of what he was looking for. Because he had a strong Australian accent, it was hard for me to understand him. His business dealt with infomercials, exercise, and nutrition. He needed an editor to go over exercise manuals and make sure the words correctly correlated with the picture of the exercise.

I accepted his offer, and we agreed on a day to get together to go over further details. The first item on the list was pay. He asked, "How much do you charge per hour in your training?" I informed him, "Fifty dollars an hour." He agreed, and I was ecstatic. I was now making fifty dollars an hour editing exercise manuals. I was doing work that I loved doing. It took me no more than four hours to complete. All he asked was that I call him when I was finished.

Coming back into the office with eagerness in his step and a smile on his face, he viewed my work. He seemed quite pleased. He wrote a check, put it in an envelope, and handed it to me. I couldn't wait to get outside and into my car so I could open it. It all felt so surreal. I was expecting two hundred dollars, but when I opened the envelope, I found it was double the amount. I screamed for joy and thanked God. One of the sayings in the Bible I remembered coming forth in my mind in this moment was how our cup overflows. My boss was so pleased with my work that he offered me a position managing, training, and basically overseeing everything that would need to be done for a televised exercise infomercial.

At this point it seemed too good to be true. But after this study was completed, the company hired me full time. My boss asked me what I would feel financially comfortable with in order to work for him. He mentioned forty thousand a year. I knew I must have had a facial expression that said, *Not so sure about that.*

I expressed to him, "Fifty thousand would sell me." I knew fifty grand a year would allow me to move out of my parents' home and find my own place. After I mentioned this amount to him, to my surprise he again agreed. I was now on my way out of my parents' home and embarking on a career. Two more dreams crossed off my list: working in the TV field and making fifty thousand dollars a year.

Within those years, I was able to not only grow my individual freedom but also my business. I was a single divorced woman with three children relying on me, finally free of my ex-husband and having a real sense of accomplishment.

2010—Owning My Own Home/ Hiring an Interior Designer

By 2005 I had achieved my SUV, personal training, twenty dollars an hour, a career earning fifty thousand dollars a year, and working in the TV field. As stated earlier my career making fifty thousand a year allowed me to move out of my parents home into a place of my own. From 2006–2010, I rented a place to live. I attempted a couple of times to look at purchasing either a single family home or a townhome.

Everyone told me they required two years proof of income because I was self-employed. When I first started looking for a place of my own it was 2008. My first two years of income were too low to get what I was looking for. So I allowed a year to go by before I searched again. In 2009, I began to search more seriously. I had done well financially that year. The year before that hadn't been the best, but it was still better than previous years.

Banks gave me a price range for houses that would fall into my financial bracket. I didn't like what they were saying, and I certainly wasn't going to settle for the price range they gave me. It just didn't serve my needs. I knew what I wanted, and I knew that somehow, someway I would get it. And I would get it with one year of documentation, not two. I knew what I could afford. I had always done well with managing my money, whether I made eight, fifteen, twenty, or twenty-five dollars an hour. My father taught me to never put all my eggs in one basket.

As I was driving down Route 40 one day, a new development caught my eye. There were townhomes, single family homes, and twin homes starting in the low $220s. I stopped with an interest in a townhome.

A sweet young male salesman greeted me with a firm handshake and asked, "What can I do for you today?"

I told him, "I am looking for a townhome or a twin home in the hopes of operating my business from it." He showed me the layout of both homes. I was excited because the layout of the townhome precisely fit my needs. We started the process immediately.

I soon found out the mortgage broker I would be working with was one I knew from years before when I first attempted to get a loan. To me it was a sign. It was the right place, the right people, the right house, the right time.

The loan officer soon told me I needed two years' worth of income documentation and twenty percent down.

"No can do," I said to him. I may have had enough to put 20 percent down, but it was all I had.

I couldn't believe it, but he said, "You have enough money, Barb."

I proclaimed, "I may, but it's all of it. You're not taking all of my money."

I was disheartened. I made a phone call to the salesman who had been taking care of me. He informed me of another bank they used to help home buyers.

About a week later, I was in a nutrition store when he called to tell me good news. He said this bank would accept one year of income documentation.

"Are you serious?" I asked. "Don't go playing games with me."

He said he was positive.

"Okay," I said. "But don't be calling me back and saying the bank changed their mind."

"I'm positive," he proclaimed.

I almost literally jumped for joy. I was a very happy woman in that moment. He gave me the contact name and number of the other bank so I could connect with them. Yes, this was happening! This was my first time ever doing anything like this. At forty-five years of age, I was buying my first home. This was also the year the government gave first-time home buyers an eight thousand dollar credit. I made that on time too. I felt like I was in heaven.

My brand new home had three bedrooms, three and a half baths, and a full finished rec room. I was approved for an additional loan amount that I could use for upgrades to add on. And that I did. Normally the bathroom in the rec room was just a powder room, so I upgraded it to a full bath. This was the room I intended to use as my business room. I also upgraded my bedroom bathroom to a suite bathroom. My kitchen normally came with vinyl flooring, so I decided to get hardwood floors in both the kitchen and the powder room just off the kitchen.

An upgrade to carpet was also in order. In addition, the house normally came with basic black or white appliances, so I upgraded those to stainless steel. Another addition I made was for two additional cable outlets and two ceiling fans. It was fun to play. And you know what, guys? Right after I was in my home, I was approached by an interior designer. I hired him to start working immediately on my business/massage room.

2010—Hiring a House Cleaner

Within the first six months of living in my new home, I hired someone to clean my house every week. Now all of the dreams I wrote down in June of 2001 were accomplished.

So, my dear ones, always think big, dream big, and never give up. Always believe in yourself. Always be guided from your spirit within. Think fruitful, positive thoughts. Focus your intentions on goodness. You are the creator of your own life. Work with yourself and along with the universe. It can only bring you what you put out.

CHAPTER 10

Hiding Behind My Hands, Afraid To Speak

When I was a child, I was afraid of talking. I feared speaking. Sometimes I feared not speaking, but not speaking was easier, so that's what I did. I hid behind my hands. I will explain more as I go along.

I was often teased because of my shyness. When I look back now, it's hard to imagine I was ever that way. It was so sad to feel so sheltered. It wasn't like I wasn't an attractive girl or that I never had any friends, for I was attractive and I did have friends. I just stayed within myself. I saw myself not just as a shy little girl, but I saw myself, knowing there was a sweet, beautiful spirit that lived inside of me, inside the body I carried around. It was like I was aware of both of my selves at the same time, but I was afraid to show the real me. I knew me. I loved me, or at least I knew I wanted to love me.

At thirteen, my body looked more like sixteen because of my breast size. I rarely spoke with other adults. When I did speak, it was mostly with my closest friends or my younger sister. The neighbor's dad teased me about being shy. He would say, "Cat got your tongue?" I was not particular to those words coming out of his mouth. I wanted to duct tape his mouth shut so I would never hear them again. He would look at my breasts as he said these words. I think his son had a crush on me; the son had two sisters, one older and one younger. The older one was a cheerleader, and I remember watching her practice her cheerleading moves. The younger sister, Kelly, was my best friend. I loved her and thought of her as the most beautiful girl I had ever seen. She had such beautiful long, dark hair and gorgeous emerald green eyes. This family also had American Indian blood. I remember that because I was proud of my own American Indian heritage. Whenever I played cowboys and Indians, I played an Indian.

My friend Kelly and I were skipping down our newly paved street one spring day, holding hands as sweet friends do, when I told her that when I grew up I would name my little girl Kelly. I admired her so much that I wanted to name my daughter after her. As you already know, I did just that many years later in 1991. I remember my friend Kelly and me making mud pies as children. Do you remember making mud pies as a kid? Or snow angels? Building Eskimo houses? I loved my snow angels. I would stand up with eyes closed while the sun was shining on my cold nose, and I would fall backward. I laid my arms out to my sides in the snow and moved them to make the angel's wings. Then I would bask in the glory, settling into a deep trance of beauty.

I think angels must have been watching over me as a child, loving me and protecting me, allowing me to remember and not remember certain things. I was so small when the sexual abuse happened that I did not remember anything. A friend of mine recently commented on why he thought I never wanted to hug my father later in life, why I only felt safe hugging my mom. What he said made sense to me, which is interesting because I had never put it together until he made the following comment: "You probably didn't want to hug your father because if you did it would have brought back memories of the abuse."

I rarely heard my father say the words *I love you*. I think he used them twice, and each of those instances were because he had come to me with real feelings. He had shown sincere emotion. It felt good to actually hear my father say, "I love you," directly to me, his daughter. I was nineteen or twenty at the time.

I grew up with much hatred toward my father, and it wasn't until 2008, after he had triple bypass surgery, that the path of loving him and forgiving him started. I knew I wanted love and forgiveness to happen within me toward my father before he passed. There were too many years of hatred directed toward him for the many things he said and did to my brothers, sisters, me, and my mom. He seemed to care for only one person, and that was himself.

The last I saw him cry was when he found out his brother had killed himself. Whenever I saw my father cry, I couldn't help but cry too. It was like I felt part of his pain. Just like when he was dying. I literally felt his spirit leave his body.

But let's go back to me hiding behind my hands as a child. What I would do was rub my hands around each other while holding them close to my belly, face or my heart. When I rubbed my hands in front of me, around and around and around, I was shielding myself from hurt. I was scared to voice myself. I only voiced when I felt happiness because that was safe. I had learned from my past that voicing myself in any other way would only create more hurt from my father. I had learned by watching how he treated my brothers and sisters.

My younger sister, who was two and a half years my junior, seemed to have no fear of voicing herself. But the thing was, she always got into trouble because of it. I learned quickly that voice equals hurt. There were many occasions when his frustration and anger were unjustified. The truth is, anger is never justified. The energy used in anger is not worth all the negative feelings that surface. For years I hid behind my hands. I hid behind my shyness. It masked all of the feelings and emotions welling up inside of me for years. It wasn't until the end of seventh grade that I made an intention to become less shy over the summer so that when I entered eighth grade I would make more friends.

When I become determined, I do what is required until it is accomplished, whatever the task may be. Even if my shyness moved just an inch forward, it was a step in the right direction. Each year that went by, I reaffirmed my dedication to becoming less shy. I took it one day at a time. Sometimes we need to take things one minute at a time.

High school sports were a disaster for me every year. I just wanted to be able to have fun without having anyone tease me. I didn't care for sports. When we were dividing into teams, I was one of the ones chosen near the end. How humiliating that was for me as a teenager. It made me feel stupid. I felt that I was no good. I felt that people thought I could not run, catch a ball, or throw a ball. I thought they believed I was too slow or too fat. I was constantly hiding, hiding from so many fears, hiding from so many things I wanted to do or say. Interestingly, many years later I would compete not only in amateur bodybuilding competitions but in swimsuit, beauty, and figure competitions. The hiding was starting to disappear during my competition days.

There were other moments when I hid behind my hands as a child. The neighborhood where I lived reminded me of a campground because there were plenty of trees to climb and roads to ride my bike on. I loved riding up and down hills, free as a bird. I would dare myself to take my hands from the handlebars and feel the air brush against my body. Me, my little sister, and my best friend, Kelly, would climb the sappy trees and make mud pies. I would pretend the tree was my tent and I was the little Indian girl. It was so much fun to get away, to play and be free of the things that went on inside my house. Outside I was free to let my spirit play.

I had another neighbor who lived at the end of my street, around the corner in a little white house with fence wrapped around it. This neighbor was a sweet, gentle little old lady who had a cute little dog with an annoying bark. All of the neighborhood children loved her, and she loved all of them. We called her the lollipop lady. She had lollipops for us, but in order for us to receive them, we had to show our manners by asking politely. Once we received the lollipops, we had to express our gratitude by saying thank you. It was fun to go visit her.

But as a child who hid behind my hands, afraid to speak, I was petrified to say please and thank you. I always held my hands close to my heart, curling them around each other. My pleases and thank-yous came out in a soft, quiet voice. The lollipop lady always asked me to speak up because she could not hear me. Being the scared little girl I was, I had to open my mouth again and utter the words, *thank you* and *please*. The lollipop lady responded, "You're welcome, dear." Then off my friend and I would go, merrily on our way, skipping hand-in-hand. I was satisfied with myself and proud that I had said thank you.

When I was in elementary school, I was afraid to raise my hand to let my teacher know that I had to use the bathroom. I was so afraid that I just wouldn't ask. Instead of fighting through this fear, I would wet my pants. When the teacher found out what had happened, she had the school nurse call my mom to come pick me up from school and take me home.

The times I did something wrong, my mom told my father. When this happened, he would get his belt and whip me on my bottom. It didn't happen very often because my father considered me the good girl, little Miss Perfect. But each time I did get whacked, my body had an automatic response. My bladder would release everything inside it.

The last time I ever got whipped by my father was when I was in tenth or eleventh grade. I asked my mom if I could go over to one of my friends' houses after school, but she said no. I had completed what I needed to do for school, so I figured I would be allowed to go. When she said no, I became upset and left for a walk. Once I started walking, I didn't want to stop. I just kept going and going and going. It started out as an act of anger, to blow off steam, but as I kept walking, it turned into a brisk walk.

I walked out of the development and onto the main road of Route 273. I decided to turn down Appleton Road, which headed in the direction of my school. I walked close to eight miles. Shortly after 5:00 p.m., my dad passed me on the road as he was driving home from work. I was thinking, *Oh shit. He saw me.* Just before he passed, in my mind I had heard me speaking to me, saying, *"Turn around, Barbara, and head back home now!"* But I didn't listen to my inner voice, and I kept walking.

I saw him back his car toward me. He rolled his window down and yelled at me to get in the car, which I did. He continued to yell at me, accusing me of skipping school even though school dismissed at 2:50 p.m. On top of that, it was after 5:00 p.m., and I was walking in the direction of the school, not away from it. I remember thinking how ridiculous it was for my father to accuse me of skipping out of school. I sat there in the car, saying nothing the entire drive home. Upon arriving home, I went up to my bedroom to read.

As I engrossed myself in the story, I heard a knock on my door. Both of my parents were there, my dad with belt in hand and my mom just standing there as she listened and watched my father beat me with it. He yelled at me again, accusing me of skipping school when I knew I hadn't. I couldn't say anything. If I had, it would not have made a difference. It was no use wasting my energy, so I took the beating. I prayed inside, thinking, *Please, God, don't let me pee my pants. Please don't let this happen again. I'm too old for this.* But once that belt hit me, the floodgates opened, and my bladder emptied all over the bed. I felt humiliated and ashamed. I couldn't believe this had happened at the age of seventeen. Moments after he left, I shed many tears.

Communication rarely happened in our home, if ever. It was simple *talk.* I never remember my parents talking with us about life. Words were empty, with no meaning or substance. There were no life lessons. Basically we all fended for ourselves and did our chores. It was rare to receive love from my father. He never said the words *I love you* to anyone. I don't remember ever hearing my father say *I love you* to my mom or my mom say *I love you* to my dad. As I look back on moments of my past, it is hard to believe that I am the person I am right now. I hid behind my hands and voice for a very long time.

When I met my future husband, I couldn't wait to get out of my parents' house. I couldn't wait to get away from my father. I couldn't wait to get away from the way he treated all of us. Little did I know that I was walking out of one dysfunctional home and into another. I don't know if my father ever hit my mother. I think it was similar to what I encountered with my husband, emotional and mental.

Many people believe sexual abuse is intercourse, but it has a wide range of behavior. Anything done in a sexual way without consent of another individual. For instance, a perpetrator imploring a minor to disrobe so he or she can see private parts is a form of sexual abuse. Any time someone feels uncomfortable with doing or saying things it is taking the side of selfishness, for love will never play into the hands of another's feelings of discomfort.

As I continued on in my life after my divorce, living with my parents, then finding my own place, and then owning my own home, I kept strong to my faith. You, my reader, have experienced some of my hard times with me, and I am thankful for you reading this book. Now as I continue to look back on my more recent life, I realize that there were many moments in which I was living behind my hands, and I would like to mention them now.

When I was a personal trainer, I enjoyed helping others change their eating patterns and their exercise regimens or lack of exercise regimens. It pleased me to see their bodies change. Their first response to me was about their sleep, how much better they were able to rest. When we take care of our bodies and minds, our spirit knows this, so our spirit becomes better. The body responds to how we feed it, how we nourish it, and how we take care of it. It is all one as we are all one. As we feed each other with loving, positive words and actions, people as a whole will flourish.

Many of my trainings were one-on-one. Then it moved into group settings with the senior citizens I helped and also the groups of people I worked with for the infomercials. I always knew I wanted and needed to have that one-on-one connection, to use my hands in my work. Each time I helped adjust a client's form to help them execute a move, the touch felt good to me. I could feel the connection. I didn't realize at the time that such a spiritual connection could or would take place. I just knew that I felt something strong. Something I wanted more of.

I would ask these hands of mine, "What do you want me to do?" It was like I was hiding behind them, hiding from my real purpose, from what I was meant to do with them. At least I knew something more was going on within my hands, which is why I asked. Times would arise when clients would comment to me that they had a sore back, shoulders, or feet. When I asked if they would like for me to rub their area of soreness, all of them welcomed it.

The personal training school I had gone to also had a massage school. I had stayed away from that on purpose because of the additional learning of muscle attachments and origins that was necessary, even though I had felt the pull to go. I chose to not go until years later. Saying no to that gentle pull was me hiding behind what I was feeling called to do; I hid out of fear. Fear of me not performing to a higher level. Fear of not viewing myself as worthy or good enough to perform such a task.

At the time my heart was set on personal training and personal training only. But having my own business and working for a company has helped me gain confidence and more belief in myself. When I was laid off from my television job, I did not know what to do. I had to come up with something fast. I thought of my hands and how I could use them to gift the income for me and my children. That was when I decided to put myself through massage training and quickly started building a massage clientele within three months of becoming a certified technician. In the state in which I resided, certification was required before one could ask for payment from clients.

I started my massage business in 2008. That same year, I came across an individual who told me about the "green books," The St. Germaine series. He let me borrow one. As I read this book, I could feel heat energy move through my body. I felt tingles and heat throughout my being. I started receiving creative ideas about certain moves to do on clients. My hands took over. They had a mind of their own. I trusted this, allowing my hands to do their work. I followed my hands rather than me, rather than allowing my brain to tell my hands what to do and where to go. It was like I was forming a piece of art out of the body that lay on my table, much like a sculptor forms his artwork out of clay.

I found that I was good at massage, so much so that several clients were surprised when they found out I had just started. They thought I had been doing it for years. I didn't feel like I was hiding behind my hands anymore.

But in 2011 I noticed I was hiding behind my hands via the computer and my home. I did not put myself out there in the public eye. I marketed my business only through the Internet, posting ads in different locations. Since I worked in my home, only once people came to see me and allowed me to service them did they see for themselves how good I was.

When I was talking to my son, Jeff, one Wednesday about me being shy as a child and hiding behind my hands, it hit me that I still was hiding behind them but in a different way. It was an interesting revelation to see me hiding behind my hands in my work. You may wonder and ask, "How do you hide behind your hands if you're already using your hands in your gift?" I will do my best to explain.

I was hiding behind the walls of my house and my hands. I was open and able to let myself fully be in my work in those moments when I was engaged in the massage. There was a part of me that hid inside the confines of the walls of my home because I was afraid of others judging me. I was concerned people would think I was weird or not understand, so I stayed behind. I judged those whom I thought would judge me.

When I was invited to be a vendor at a holistic weekend event, I checked it out and decided the time was now for me to branch out into the public instead of fully relying on the Internet. The Internet is a wonderful tool through which I have met many good people, and I will continue to market myself in such a way. The important thing was for me to recognize that I was hiding myself and my talents, my ability to truly help others on a spiritual level. I've always been a very deep person. I now feel more alive and free to be more of who I am outside of my home, that there is nothing to fear from me showing my own light. Before, I only showed in places I felt safe. It was now time for me to not hide behind my hands, to not hide behind my light.

CHAPTER 11

My Voice

The voice of a child afraid to speak, holding it inside my body, my mind and soul. Afraid to voice all of what I wanted, needed, desired and dreamed. There was so much pain within me stemming from the way my father treated me, my mom, my brothers and sisters. I did this for many years. In my teen years and into adulthood, I had an eating disorder called bulimia. I would binge and purge, abusing exercise and food to numb the pains of what was going on inside of me, knowingly and unknowingly. The eating disorder started when I was in tenth grade. I was chubby at times as I saw myself, yet I must have been attractive to the opposite sex because I was teased sexually by schoolboys or other men that would glance at me when I was at the beach or walking around wherever I happened to be walking.

I filled out my top at thirteen years of age. Men thought I was sixteen when I was thirteen because of my breast size. I don't remember how that made me feel other than pretty good to look older than my age. I don't recall how the eating disorder started or what gave me the fascination to purge the food I ate. I just knew that the eating felt good and it allowed me to halt the negative feelings I had about myself. I would exercise on my own while listening to music as I lay on the floor, doing leg lifts, donkey raises, kickbacks.

A lot of what I did was for the lower half of my body. I detested my legs, which I never quite understood. I often received compliments on my legs from many individuals, men and women. I received compliments from people who thought I was a dancer. I thought, *Me? No, not me.* Though I had wished I was a dancer because I loved to dance and I loved to watch dancing. I would visualize myself onstage, dancing for crowds while everyone stared at me, loving me, seeing my beauty and all the love inside of my being. But no, I was not a dancer.

Many times I looked down at my legs and spoke to them, saying words like, "Gross. My legs look fat." I wanted and needed to cover my legs once the cooler weather came. I felt vulnerable with bare legs. It's funny and interesting that I was fine wearing short shorts in the summer, but once cooler weather came, I felt the need to cover them up. It was a psychological thing inside me that I was aware of. Somehow I knew I wanted my legs covered. I wondered what feeling made me need that. I asked myself, "Why do you feel the need to cover your legs, Barbara?" It felt as if I had somehow been violated in my private area. I wondered about these thoughts before and after I found out I had been sexually abused.

I hid my eating disorder for years and not until after I was married did I go to my husband and tell him I suffered from this disease. No one could tell I had an eating disorder because of the type of disorder. Bulimia is not easily seen by viewing a person's body. I was a normal height and weight, and it wasn't like I ate and purged everything like you see portrayed on TV. Not all bulimics are like that. For me, it was a monthly event. Every month, something inside me got a hold of me on an emotional level, so much so that when I felt this punch in my stomach, so to say, I went to food for comfort.

Sweets were my treat and usually creamy. That, I also wondered about, the creamy sensations I wanted. I wondered if there was any correlation between the types of food I chose and the emotion I had or with what had been done to me or what I had been forced to do. Ice cream, creamy peanut butter, cookies, and cookie dough were food items I often stuffed down to soothe my pains. I pushed emotions down with food without thinking. Once I became consciously aware of how much I had eaten, I would become disgusted with myself and, following those feelings of hatred for myself and what I had done, purge them out. I would make myself throw up until I felt better, until I released these emotions out of me. At that point I would feel fine, like it was okay to go about my day. While I was pregnant I made sure to not binge and purge. I did not want to cause harm to my babies.

As I write to you now, mentioning my binge-purge cycle occurring monthly, a question comes to my mind: was it during my moon phase (menstruation) that I did this act? I don't know that answer, but I found out during counseling that nearly 75 percent of all individuals who have suffered any form of eating disorder were sexually abused at some time in their lives. In sexual abuse, the perpetrator takes away free will because they want to have control. The act of me binging and purging was me knowing that I was the one controlling my body through what I put into it or did with it. It was a sense of control because I had lost control to someone else prior. It is a scary feeling to lose control over oneself like that.

My husband seemed to enjoy blaming me for marriage mishaps. Everything was always my fault because I was the one who had been unfaithful or had a "sex problem." I was sick, so he placed the blame for all problems on me. I was the one with an eating disorder. He took no responsibility for his own actions within the marriage. But I decided one day it was time for me to face him with the truth of this disease. I spoke about it because I felt he deserved to know. For me it was humbling. But it backfired because he used it as a weapon against me.

There were several instances over the years when he remarked, "If you don't do such and such, then you don't love me." I felt damned if I did and damned if I didn't. I learned to be silent again, for speaking out had not gotten me anywhere. Silence, however, does not serve you or others in your life. But at least I didn't hear accusations from my husband as much. Being quiet kept me in the safe zone. Just like when I was a child with my father: silent equaled safe. I knew I wanted to do my best by loving my children and taking care of them the best way I knew how.

The day of and the day after my separation, boy did I have a voice! I had an angry, loud, cursing voice. I was free in the physical sense, so in my mind I felt I had the right to yell and scream and vent this anger out loud to let people know just how much I was the victim here, not my husband, who was the one crying victim. Going from having no voice to having a voice was quite the extreme. I wanted justice and payback. My heart hurt, my body ached, and my stomach was torn to shreds from so much turmoil. Underneath it all, deep within my being, I also knew that I would be okay. That I, someday, somehow, would prosper on my own with no help from a man. Having my angel loving me, watching over me, and protecting me, I knew this. Little did I know just how much I was being protected. I worked on doing the best for myself and my children considering the situation. Even though I had made mistakes along the way in my marriage and raising children, my children were my world.

I hid, holding so much inside of me; there was only so much time that could go by until I popped my head off with explosive hate toward the male population. I had felt at that time in my life that I had the right to voice my anger because I lived with so much anger toward my father and ex-husband. I had anger toward all the people in my life who wouldn't listen to the words I spoke. I had always felt that no one ever listened to me or took the time to truly care about me and my feelings, my thoughts, and my world! I always felt like I was being pushed aside like a dirty old rag for someone else to rub their dirt on. So I felt dirty on the inside and on the outside.

Self-mutilation by making myself throw up was my comforting/painful way to release emotions. People don't have to be quiet on the inside or introverted to have emptiness just because they are quiet. Many seem to be empty inside in some fashion or another. But it comes out in many forms. It could be the opposite and some people could be very loud. They may either hide their voice or express it loudly and strongly. They may bring it out through competing in whatever fashion they compete. The examples are endless, from the obvious to the less obvious. Here are a few to think about:

- Anorexia
- Bulimia
- Any drug addiction, including legalized drugs such as prescription medication, cigarettes, and alcohol
- Sports
- Work
- Children

- Control of children's sports, wanting them to be what you wanted for yourself growing up but never had or felt you somehow failed in
- Shopping
- Baking
- Cooking
- Cleaning
- Hoarding
- Loss of a loved one through death or disease
- Owning many pets
- Computer fanatics
- Watching excessive TV/movies
- Desiring to do too much in the now
- Extreme impatience
- Having to keep everything "just right"
- Missionary teachings
- Anything in excess or desire for the now, now for themselves or others

Standing up to my husband on the day of our separation, standing firm and telling my mom about the abuse, and standing up to my father about the fire was me standing strong with a voice. It was time for me to be heard. Writing this book for you is also healing and standing strong to myself. Voicing my story through the words on these pages, I stand strong to truth. I stand strong to universal truth. I stand for spiritual freedom. I stand strong for life.

Whatever situation you find yourself in, be courageous in your voice so you can start a new, blessed life. It's okay to talk to let someone know what's going on. That is the first step—recognizing that there is something there inside you that bothers you. Don't give up on you. Don't give up on others either. They need your love and support, even when it is difficult. It doesn't mean you have to physically be in the other person's life, but you can be there emotionally and spiritually.

It is difficult for the person who feels he or she is being controlled by addictions/obsessions that are overtaking him or her. Sometimes that person sees. Sometimes he or she does not. People in this situation may have so many walls up that they are unable to see through them. It may feel to them like you don't love or care about them, but the opposite is true. They need help. They do not need to be cast away, feeling lost and trapped inside their bodies. Addictions are purely a form a self-hate. It doesn't matter the addiction. The addiction fills an emotional need that is empty inside of them. It is love that they want to fill their hearts with, a love they didn't feel from their mothers or fathers or whomever their main caretakers were.

There is so much hate, distrust, anger, and loneliness inside millions upon millions of people on this Earth. It is important that we get back to loving each other. All of each other. Not just our immediate families. All people are precious and have needs they crave to fill, needs they die to have filled. Sometimes they literally die.

CHAPTER 12

Father's Sickness and Death

In 2008, my father had a major heart attack that put him in the hospital. He was informed by his doctor that he needed to have triple bypass surgery. I remember my father being scared, not knowing what to do. I certainly didn't blame him. I'd be scared too if I had to have heart surgery. But he also knew what the consequences would be if he did not have it. He would wither away and die. So he said yes to the surgery, and it went fine. I could tell my father was thankful.

After surgery, the doctors ordered him to follow a special diet of low caffeine and no sugar and to be careful of everything that went into his body. He followed his diet for a time with the help from my mother, and he was doing well. I'm not sure how long this went on before he reverted back to his old eating patterns, but the one thing that did stick was that he never smoked another cigarette.

One day when I went to visit my parents, specifically my father, he was walking with ease. He proudly stated how happy he was that he wasn't smoking. He said to me, "Barbara, I don't even crave cigarettes." I was happy and proud of him. It was in that moment that I learned to begin to love him again. There was a feeling of freedom within me. I could see in my father's eyes that he felt freedom too, so much so that we hugged and embraced one another. After this visit, each time I went to visit my parents, I always wanted to make sure to give my father a goodbye hug.

It reminded me of all those years ago when I was envious of my cousins' family when each of them hugged and kissed both of their parents. Now I had that, doing that with both of my parents.

In 2010, not too long before Thanksgiving, his health started to deteriorate again. He was becoming weak and not eating like he normally would. He was tired all of the time. To make a long story short, he ended up being admitted to the hospital. The prognosis was devastating. The doctors gave my father a choice of going home to have hospice care or staying in a hospice facility. Like my father's mother when she was ill and passed, he chose to go home. He came home on a Monday afternoon. In the remainder of this chapter, I'm going to tell you the story about what I went through during this time up until his death.

December 15, 2010

Today a sign was given to me from high above, although I didn't realize it was for me until the exact same thing happened a second time. The first time it happened was during one of my massage sessions. As I was working with my client's energy in the core of his body, I saw the presence of his grandmother, his mom's mom.

Let me preface this with the following: Anytime I perform a session longer than one hour, I set my CD player to continue playing over and over. It can be set to play one time all the way through. It can be set to play just one song over and over. Or it can be set to play the whole CD over and over. I set it to play the entire CD over and over.

As I was working, listening to the CD, working on my client's abdomen, I psychically heard, felt, and saw his grandmother. At the same time this was going on, my ears noticed that the CD was playing the same song over and over again.

I questioned myself and I actually asked my client, "You did hear 'Ave Maria,' right?" I asked about "Ave Maria" because it was a song in the middle of the CD.

He replied, "Yes."

I asked, "You are hearing this song"—a different one than "Ave Maria"—"over and over too, correct?"

He answered affirmatively. He asked, "Is there a spirit here?"

I asked him, "Is your grandmother dead?"

Again he answered affirmatively. In fact, both of his grandmothers had passed. I informed him that I felt his mom's mom and that maybe it was her messing with the electronics. Spirits have a tendency to do that to get our attention.

Spirits can do anything to get our attention. Electronics is one of the ways. I let this go with the assumption that it was her. I also noticed that it was the first song on the CD that was playing over and over. The exact same thing happened again with another client the following day. And again it was the very first song on the CD playing over and over. I took that as a sign for me, a sign that someone was helping me so I could find the answer to my question about what to do concerning visiting my father.

I wanted to know if I should go visit him at home while he was in hospice care. I interpreted the answer from the first song being played over and over on both occasions with both clients. The number one represented me, myself, and I. Me, the divine in me. I needed to look to myself, inside myself, not to the man in my life. Not to an outside source. Spirit was telling me, "Barbara, you need Barbara." I realized I didn't need to and should not rely on another person. The spirit said, "You need to go see your father! See him. Face your fear. Do not run away from this." Facing his passing was a struggle for me.

The past few days had been a struggle for me on many levels. In this answer, I was enlightened to know and feel such a strong sensation that I should go see my father and not worry about my lover. My lover needed his own time, just as I needed my own time. We both had loved ones dying. I thanked the spirit.

December 18, 2010

On the night of December 18, I went over to Mom's to visit Dad. I stayed next to his bed for almost an hour. I loved how his eyes lit up when he noticed me. They were so blue. He was loved by a lot of people, and he had given himself the way he knew how. I wondered what all was traveling through his mind, how much he had forgiven others and himself. I telepathically expressed to him loving and kind words.

As I laid my hand on top of his, he gently took his other hand and laid it on top of mine. That action moved me very much and almost brought tears to my eyes. Instead, I smiled with joy and love in my heart. I then saw a beautiful angel, as all Angels of Light are, opening up and enveloping the entire room. There was so much peace.

My Angel Bearer of Light spoke to me later that evening: "Angels comfort the sick no matter their crimes." I allowed my hands to comfort my father with gentle, loving strokes on his arms, face, and legs. I held his hand. I kissed his forehead. And I whispered in his ear several times, "I love you." This was much easier to do than I had ever thought possible.

December 19, 2010

I went to visit Dad again the next evening. Three of my sisters and one brother were there. My brother didn't stay long. I don't think he was able to bear what was going on. I saw him dart upstairs and heard his cries of pain and sadness. I wondered what was going on inside his mind and body. He left shortly afterward.

It was evening, and I lay down on my mom's couch, tired from my day. I didn't know how long I had been lying there, but I suppose it was an hour or so. I suddenly awoke around 9:30 p.m. and felt energy leave my father. I could feel the pull coming from deep inside my belly and in my heart. I felt the shift of his spirit energy going down and out. He was still alive. It was simply an energy I felt from him.

Two tears rolled down out of the corner of my right eye. I held my tears inside as long I could, leaving briskly after this event. I knew it was time to go home for many reasons. I did not want anyone to see me like this because I knew they would not be able to understand. It was energy, energy I was sensitive to. It would be too hard for me to explain all of this to my family.

I was aware and watchful of myself with my eating habits during this time. I needed to feel my emotions and not stuff them down with food. I worked through this and had to work through this for my inner being to transform. I had to transform. I was being transformed. Everything had to come from the right place, the divine place. It is interesting how I feel these shifts, the movement of energy. It is good. And it is very good that I am aware.

December 20, 2010

I went over my Mom's again the following night. I did not sit long with Dad. It was hard to watch his eyes glazing over. Death was very near. The nurses said it was the medicine. They had increased it to help him with the pain. It was hard seeing how fast he went down, even though I knew it.

I spent most of the time in the living room and kitchen. Two of my mother's sisters were there, along with my sister Lynette. Everyone seemed to have accepted his nearing death, for all were talking and eating with what appeared to be happy faces.

When I got home that night and was all comfortable and snuggled in my bed, fast asleep in dream state, I felt a major shift. I felt his spirit fully move out of his body and feel freedom and release. I in turn also felt it.

All day of Monday, December 20, 2010, had been tough for me because I could constantly feel my dad's energy shifting before its full release. There were many tears. I also knew in my heart that I needed to be one of the family members to speak at his celebration of life.

December 21, 2010

After one of my goddess sessions, I saw that my brother-in-law had left a message on my phone. I listened to it, but I already knew what he was going to say. My dad had passed. I soon left to go comfort my mom.

December 29, 2010

The day of the ceremony to celebrate the life of my father came. Since we had grown up Catholic, it took place in a Catholic church. I have heard that once spirits pass out of the body, they attend their own service. Well, I definitely felt my father later at home where we held the gathering of friends and family.

In our living room, Mom had her couches and many chairs to sit on. Everyone was talking and eating food from paper plates. I was standing next to my cousin Michael. He was talking to me about his and his fiancé's wedding plans. As I listened to him, I felt my father standing next to me, giggling. He was walking around, playing, listening to everyone's conversation.

He walked back over to me again and stood next to me, letting me know the fun he was having. I smiled and laughed. I expressed to my cousin, "I feel Dad now." Dad seemed to be enjoying himself walking around, checking everyone, and listening to conversations. That was the only time I ever felt him.

Father's Eulogy

Here is the eulogy I spoke at my father's celebration of life:

I am having some beautiful memories of me with my dad. I will write as I remember. They each make me smile so big with complete and utter joy! Such an opening of my heart that is indescribable and just plain beautiful.

Every Easter my mom would put our Easter baskets together. After my younger sister and I went on our search and found our baskets, we would see what all we received. The most fun part of all of this was in the morning when we woke up. When I opened my eyes, one of the first things I saw was a note from Dad. Each note was a step of what to do next. A bunny trail it was. Oh, what fun. I don't remember too much of what each said but here are some examples:

a) Take ten steps forward.
b) Take two hops and then three steps to the right.
c) Go down the steps, around the corner, and look behind the sofa.

Some were pictures of bunny paws leading us to the next note of where to go until we finally found our baskets. It was so much fun. I followed the notes, doing everything that it said to do in much anticipation of reaching the final destination. And oh boy, when I reached the final destination, what joy to really see all that was in our Easter baskets. Even the colors of the cellophane wrap. There was pink and green and violet. I loved all of it. Me and my sister would receive white chocolate, milk chocolate, jellybeans, robin eggs, malt balls, a hollow chocolate Easter bunny, and always a stuffed bunny.

*Another moment of time with Dad was sitting on his lap at
the dinner table, giving me a ride on his knee like a horse. To
feel the jiggle, the bumps along the ride making me giggle. If
I didn't outwardly giggle, I was giggling on the inside.*

*At the dinner table during our meal, I remember my father walking his
fingers over to me and my sisters, getting our hands, checking to see if we
were done. That is, if we were done cooking. It was cute and silly.*

*Another moment was at Christmas when I was twelve and he bought me a
ten-speed bicycle. I was so excited. I couldn't wait to ride it. There is a picture
somewhere of that Christmas, and he's kneeling down next to me while I'm
opening a gift. That was special. I felt love from his heart going to mine in that
memory. There really are many memories of happiness. Dad enjoyed giving of
himself in the form of gift giving. I didn't see so much so then, but now as I
know and I have learned more about life and love, I have come to know this
was my father's way of showing his love to his family: the act of gift giving.*

*Each of us has our own way of giving love and receiving love. I am thankful
and grateful for so much more now, for everything he really did do and tried
to do to show his love to all of us. May he be in peace as angels watch over him.*

If you died today, what would you do? How would you be? How is it
you would treat yourself and others? None of us know when that time will
come, but we all know it will come! Where is the majority of your energy
spent? Are you loving? Are you really loving with all of who you are? And if

not, why? Fear of showing emotions, feelings? Thoughts of what others may think of you? Are you allowing ego to get in the way? There are always so many questions we can ask ourselves to find out where we are in our lives, why we do what we do.

Why we don't do things, I believe, is an even more important question we must ask ourselves. Most of the time it's what we are *not* doing verses what we are doing. In order to find all the answers to your questions about yourself, about the way you think and are, you must go inside yourself, to your spirit, for that is where the answers lie. There is a place inside of you in which only love exists. Don't procrastinate! You can save yourself.

You can live as an enlightened being or not. The choice is yours. If you willingly choose a state of enlightenment, you will have to make choices in order for you to change. Yes, change is required. Change from the state you have been so used to all of your life, a state of misbeliefs and even outright lies. Building spiritual strength takes time. It takes loving yourself throughout it all, throughout the times you make mistakes, not purposefully but because of what you have been so used to for so long.

So, my dear reader, I plead for you to know that forgiveness is a spiritual duty. It has nothing to do with accepting any evil forced on us as victims. We must accept this spiritual duty and then live it; otherwise, you take the Creator's role of judgment. And when I say the word *judgment*, this does not mean that our Creator judges us, for our Creator does not judge or condemn us. Our Creator loves us and can only create. I said the *role of judgment*, which basically means our circle of life.

In the end, we judge ourselves. Our Creator does not judge. Our Creator presents to us our whole lives when we "die" and leave our bodies. We must humble ourselves, ask for forgiveness, in order to be cleansed and purified of all our wrongs before we can enter into the light. We will always get back what we put out, whether our works are good or evil, positive or negative. We must release and forgive or we will perish spiritually. It is important for us to purify our inner selves before we can move outward.

If we know something to be true, then we must live it. Like the old saying goes, "If you cannot live it, then don't preach it." I personally strive to mean what I say and say what I mean. Before my father passed out of his body, I came to love and forgive him.

CHAPTER 13

Meditation Commitments

Commitment. What does it mean? What does it represent to you? When you hear the word, what does it feel like to your heart, mind, and body? It appears that many people fear committing to their relationships. It is easier to be committed to a job, volunteer work, a hobby, or an extracurricular activity. These are well and good on a superficial level, and they can help you get where you want to go professionally and socially, but I would like to pose a question to you regarding the commitments you may have with others, whether it be with your mate or anyone else for that matter.

When we commit, it is not a commitment in which we feel required to tell the other person everywhere we are going, with whom we are spending time, or when we will be back. Some people think commitment equals control. But it is quite the opposite. Commitment is about loving ourselves enough to *want* to give to others in such ways as letting the others know what's going on in our lives. It's a commitment to the love you have for them and for you. When you love yourself, you commit yourself to the duty of being good and right in your mind through thoughts and actions. Many people claim to be honorable, but they are not. Many people claim to love, but they don't. People claim so many things, but often, when it gets down to the nitty-gritty, people show another side.

It is important to have concern for others and for ourselves. Ultimately we live and will die with everything we have done or said to ourselves and others. At the end of the day, it's important that we have lived in honor to all, not the select few we want to choose because it's easier for us. Commit to the divine Angels of Light. Commit to love. Commit to spirit, every day with gratitude. We must never forget to be thankful. When we feel we are in a funky mood, it is because we need a gratitude check.

It appears to me, from what I have seen with my own eyes, so many people think the word and act of *commitment* equals control. Commitment does not equal control. I would guess that everyone realizes control definitely doesn't equal commitment. There is so much fear in love, in commitment, in honesty. Fear we will not be heard, be validated, be cared for, be believed and fear of rejection. For me, I'd rather not waste time. I am who I am, all of me, all real, all love. Anytime I am in a relationship with someone, a romantic relationship, I am committed to that person. I came to realize and know that when I was unfaithful to my husband I didn't love him. I realized I married him for the wrong reason. I married because I was in love with love. I was in love with the idea of love. I have forgiven him and myself. I now love me fully.

However, my commitment is not necessarily to that person. It is a commitment to the love I have for that person. Commitment to my husband broke down when my love for him did. Yet I also came to realize that I never loved him because I never knew how to love me. The love I have for me now is so great for myself that when I find joy in being with a person, I automatically commit, so they automatically receive a commitment from me. There is a difference. Because I love me, all the love I possess within me, it is easy for me to give 110 percent of myself. For me, it's a given. It's just me, because relationships are the foundation of a healthy, harmonious world. Not only do I think of it in terms of us, the two people involved, but it is bigger and wider than that. It expands outward to all of our surroundings; it affects everyone around us on a national and, yes, even global level. Love has no end. Love has no beginning. Love *is*. It just is. Love is letting go of fear.

After everything I have been through, I find it absolutely amazing, almost miraculous, that I in fact have so much love to give. I have actually grown the love within me. And deep down I know that no one can take that away. No one can control my spirit. They may hurt me with words, actions, or lack of actions, but never have I given up on real love, divine love, love that comes from deep within our hearts and souls.

Now let's return to the topic of commitment and people's idea that somehow commitment equals control, that once you commit yourself to someone, you *have* to tell that person everything: where you're going, what you're doing, who you're with, when you'll be back, how long you'll be gone, etc. If that is what you feel is expected of you, you might be right or you might be wrong, but you really don't know what is going on inside another person's mind. We all have free will, and we all have free choice. We choose to believe what we want to believe, sometimes without fully understanding the other person's thought process.

I think this is where we get into so much trouble. Each person is now thinking, "You don't love me" or "You don't care for me" or "You're not here" or "Just what are you doing?" It's more about what the person is *not* doing than what they *are* doing. It could be that you are in a pretty darn good relationship, but there is something ever so small that is missing. Maybe it's the lack of what they are not doing and the fact that what they are not doing is actually so very easy and simple to fix.

We all know how men love to fix things that are broken. They receive joy and satisfaction in fixing things or doing something to fix a situation. You hear, "Honey, just tell me what you want and I'll do it." Men want and enjoy making their women happy, but yet it appears that anytime women show any emotion, men interpret that as being needy or clingy. Then women react and think, *You don't love me. You don't care! If you really loved me, you would care to understand my tears.* Or the man might say, "If you loved me, you wouldn't have a problem having sex with me." The constant blame gets passed back and forth, back and forth until someone walks away or storms out the door. Now instead of being better, it's worse.

So where does commitment fall into this? A commitment is being strong enough to stay and face *your* own stuff. It is being strong enough by not allowing ego or arrogance to get in the way. It is about becoming humble and at least attempting to look at what the other person is saying. Take a good look at yourself instead of playing the blame game or constantly criticizing, condemning, and judging. There is no love in that. There is only fear.

So many people leave at the first sign of trouble. Or if it was not the first sign of troubling times, why did they not speak up? If they did speak up, then why is it still happening? You could go around and around and around thinking and even saying, "Well, you need to change. Well, I'm not changing until you change." But honestly, this is a cop-out. It is a cop-out to yourself, your self-awareness, and your self-respect.

How many of us even know what self-love, self-respect, or self-acceptance really looks like? We have been handed down other people's beliefs and perceptions of what this means. We have, I feel, become desensitized to the true meaning.

When you desire to know and learn what divine self-love is about, all else falls into place with ease. This starts the path of everything becoming easier. As you learn and grow through your mistakes and the mistakes of others, you become more aware of your true identity, your soul, your spirit. We are all spirits, and this is where all good resides. It is within you. Have the commitment to your divine self. Let the other person have his or her commitment to his or her divine self. That is the starting point. Work together from there. Not the physical self, the divine self.

Do you know you have a divine self? In order to start, you need to know that you have one. It is the white light inside you. That is your spirit. All light is all love. Light feeds light. The darkness of your past cannot feed light.

Think for a moment of white and black, light and dark. Picture in your mind these two forces coming together, meeting one another. Take out a piece of paper and draw a line down the middle of it. To the left side is all white. To the right side is all black. Now imagine the white moving into the black. The black becomes gray in color. It starts to dissipate. Move the white over farther into the black until all of the black is gray. Your dark clouds start to lift and become easier to deal with. Your mind starts to open, and you see more of the shadows in your life, shadows you have the power to completely banish from existence.

Now add more white to the gray until the gray becomes a lighter shade and the shadows lift even more. Life is again easier to deal with. Your life becomes awake and more alive. The more you focus on your light, the more you become free of past pains and hurts. When you feel a certain negative way toward yourself or another, recognize it, face it. When you face it, you have the power to push through it. Yes, it can be difficult to push through these moments, but it is all worth it. Do something constructive to push through these times. Some people talk to themselves using affirmations and mantras. I will go into this more in a later chapter. For now, feel your shifts. See your shifts.

The dark color and shades of gray cast a shadow. Our commitments to ourselves, to others, to our mates, and to our loved ones require an open door through which we can express what we see might be going on in them. Then the commitment lies in the other person to look at it for themselves, to love themselves enough, to honor themselves and their mates by just looking. Be careful not to look at the other person in a criticizing way or as being mean. It is an observation. So much of it is in how we word things, our tone, and our body language. Reflect back and forth with the other person so you understand what has been said. Mirror. Commit to that. Remember, fear does not serve you. Humbleness does. I will end by saying, embrace and love the word *commitment*. It is a gift you give yourself and all those in your life. It says *I do*.

Feel free to use the meditations below to help you be in a committed state of love and forgiveness. May you feel and be blessed because of them.

Invocation/Benediction

An invocation and benediction that I sometimes use for myself, if you wish to use it for yourself, goes as follows:

Invocation for Self

I recognize and know that I am what I am, that God's spirit dwells in me at all times. Universal life force is with me, all around me, working on my behalf at all times for my good. I am love. I am peace. I am spirit. I am unconditional love. I know that all of us are united as one cosmic source, and I am thankful for this knowing. I embrace it and use it for the good in me and all in my life.

Benediction for Self

I am so grateful for your presence, for giving me this day, for blessing me with all who enter my life—the young and the old, new faces, new friends, and new experiences to grow and expand upon. Bless all those who have entered into my life today. Bless all those who have given thought of me today. I acknowledge all that is and all that is to become.

If you and another are meditating together, here is an invocation and benediction that you may want to use:

Invocation with Partner

We sit here gathered together today spirit recognizing_____ (insert person's name) as an indwelling spirit, the inner source being that knows all, infinite supply of life. I recognize this source within _____ (insert person's name) and within me. Be with us, spirit, as we go through our meditative process. Keep us one with you. We know everyone is united by one cosmic source. Thank you for this knowing, blessing us now and through this meditation. Thank you for me. Thank you for_____(insert person's name). Thank you for allowing this day to come forth in our lives. And we say, and so it is.

Benediction with Partner

Thank you. We are so grateful for your presence today in this meditation service. Bless _____ (insert person's name) today as he/she goes about his/her day in whatever capacity he/she chooses. Keep him/her safe in all his/her journeys. Spirit, we know the continual flow of blessings is a part of our lives. We allow us to be free of who we are. We allow ourselves to be available and willing vessels for our higher good. Open our minds and bodies. We complete our meditation service by saying, and so it is.

Meditation

The following are two examples of meditations I have been through. I hope they serve you well.

Love Meditation for Self

Sit cross-legged on your bed, with palms facing upward over your knees. Close your eyes and start with a slow, deep inhale breath. Breathe in through your nose to a count of five, and breathe out to a count of five. Do this at least five times. Then focus on your heart chakra and continue soft, gentle breathing, always inhaling and exhaling through your nose so the energy stays inside your body.

As you continue to feel in your heart, think of the love you have for your spirit. Feel you. See you. Stay here in this spot, with your heart, feeling you and loving you, until you feel a deep sense of gratitude for all that you are and all that you have. From here, focus the love you have for you out into the heart of another. In this moment, you can choose to have your thoughts directed toward a certain person or even to a certain group of people, or if you would like, to a business community for which you have heartfelt concerns. Take another deep breath, inhaling and exhaling through your nose, feeling and knowing that all of this love you have within yourself is going forward to the person or group of people to whom you are sending it. Trust in this. Know that this is happening right here and right now.

Feel the love for yourself as you take this energy from your heart down a level into the solar plexus and feel here. Stay settled in this moment for a few minutes before traveling down into the sex chakra, breathing in through your nose and out through your nose. All love energy. Feel peace. Once you feel loving peace in your sex chakra, then take it down into the root chakra, and do the same thing here. Always take nice long, slow deep breaths in and long, slow exhale breaths out of your nose.

Once you settle in here for a few moments, keeping and feeling the love in your root chakra, shoot that love energy up your spine and into your head like a bolt of lightning. Universal life force is within you. It is not just around you but within you at the same time. Use this life force for you. Once you have shot this energy throughout your body, from roots up to crown and out of your body, bring it back into your heart and be more filled with the loving peace you are now in. Say thank you to all love and light beings. It is not necessary to know their names. Thanksgivings are simple. All you need to say is, "Thank you, spirits of love and light." It is truly that simple. Then thank yourself.

I would like you to know that allowing yourself to receive this heart opening can be as powerful for you as you make it. Practice as often as you wish. To begin, you may read this mediation slowly, feeling the words. Do this as many times as you wish until you remember how and can do it without the book.

Love Meditation with Partner

Before you and the one you are with start your meditation, I want each of you to have your own candle. You may choose to either sit side-by-side or across from each other. With candle in front of you, light it. (I recommend a wide base jar candle so you do not have to hold anything) Gaze into the flame. Focus your eyes and thoughts onto the flame. Envision your body inside the flame. This flame of light that burns is inside your being; the light within you burns. Note the colors you see in the flame, and envision them inside of you.

We as humans are able to easily see the physical candle and flame in front of us. We can see the different colors within the flame. We know blue is the hottest part of the flame and is closest to the wick. We can see other colors such as yellow and orange. And if you look closely enough as you gaze upon the flame, you can see green. Let your mind envision all of the colors of the rainbow within this flame. As you see all of these colors, take this and put it inside the flame you have envisioned within your body. See it, feel it, know it is there. The white light within you is filled with all the colors of the rainbow. They are a part of you. These colors are what make the white light inside of you.

Inhale a deep breath through your nose, and take this air down inside of you as you exhale out through your nose. Then inhale through your nose and pull it up as you exhale, feeling all the colors of your white light sink down inside of you, settling in the core of your body, in your belly, solar plexus, and heart. Throughout this whole region is your flame. This is the light that burns inside you. This is your spirit within you. Take another deep, long, slow inhale and exhale, feeling the flame, feeling your light. You may feel this flame of light more in the front of your body, or you may feel it more toward the back of your body, behind your spine. You may be able to feel it throughout you, in the front and the back of your body at the same time.

If you only feel it in the front or the back of your body, visualize the rainbow colors of your white light in the front and the back at the same time. Your white light spirit within you does not get bigger or wider. It is only your mind that perceives it that way. Once you open your spirit and your mind, you are able to see more, you are able to know more. Because you are able to see and know more, the truth is there for you to tap into and use for the benefit of your soul and your life.

If it any point during this meditation your body feels the need to do a certain thing, then do it. For example, you might feel the need to move your arms, your hands, or your fingers, flowing with the universal energy of life. It is like your body moves with the energy of your spirit, and your spirit moves with the energy of the universe. You become one with the universe, and you dance. You will feel lighter, almost as if you are floating above the floor in this beautiful, sweet flow of energy vibration. You will feel more peaceful. You will feel more love. You will be able to feel the love of the other person who is there with you, whether he or she is sitting next to you or across from you.

If you do feel this love from the other person, dance with his or her love. You are dancing with yourself, you are dancing with the energy vibrations of the universe, you are dancing with the love energy of the other person, and you are dancing with the other person. There is no physical contact between the two of you. It is an energy contact. All becomes one.

Breathe in through your nose and exhale through your nose, keeping this energy flow moving fluidly, smoothly, like the gentle waves of the ocean or the gentle breeze caressing you, loving you, surrounding you, enveloping your body, the other person's body, both of your bodies. The energy moves in a big circle around each of you as individuals and in a circle around both of you together, bonding with the universe, making love with the universe.

Allow your subconscious mind to drift deeper into that universal force field of light and love. It's like you are fully aware without being aware. Make note in your mind of any colors or visions that come to you. Just be aware of everything. And then if you want to write it down afterward, do so immediately when you come out of meditation.

Always thank the spirits when you finish your meditation. Thank yourself and thank the other person who is with you, as you have just enjoyed the dance of spiritual love. This ends the meditation.

After your meditation, I recommend opening space for the two of you to share with each other any questions or revelations. If you feel you want to document your revelations, experiences, visions, thoughts, or anything else, write it down. It is always interesting to go back and read what you experienced.

I also recommend setting a timer for at least twenty minutes during the meditation. If playing some light music helps your mood, go ahead and do that too. I personally like to do my meditations in silence and or with my drum. Sometimes I will play my drum and use it as my meditation. Sometimes I will play my drum for a few minutes before a meditation. Go with what feels right for you.

As you are in your meditation, consciously be aware of any colors, people, animals, circles or triangles, graphs, geometric shapes, etc., etc. Everything that you see means something. Do not discount anything. For instance, I have learned from my Angel Bearer of Light that triangles are simply pyramids that represent invisible communication. Circles represent you bonding with the universe. The butterfly represents eternity. A snake represents a threat of some kind. My Angel Bearer of Light has informed me the meaning of the following colors: yellow represents unconditional love, orange learning lessons, red faith, blue knowledge, pink creativity, purple spiritual healing, white purity. Black represents change. It is the transition between each color of the rainbow. Even though we can not see the color black in between does not mean it is not there. Death also represents change. The color green represents a border created by fear. The shade of green does not matter; it simply represents borders created by fear. Spirals will always be counter clockwise. If it spirals inward, it means death. If it spirals outward, it means birth. Do not think of this literally. It could have several meanings. For example, an outward spiral could mean the birth of a relationship or the birth of a job, new beginnings, or a new thought pattern the spirit world will give to you. An inward spiral would be the opposite; it could mean the death of a relationship, the death of a job, or the death of a fear. It is up to you to go within yourself and decipher what these basic meanings are for you in your life. Give yourself the authority to determine what your meditations and dreams are telling you about you.

CHAPTER 14

Divinity

An Angelic Experience

At the end of 2007 when I was laid off from a well-paying job, I had my first angelic experience in which physical objects were moved. This was my first career job, the one that paid me fifty thousand dollars a year working in the TV field. I was in love with the work I was doing, and I was heading in the right direction professionally.

When I received the news that they were letting me go, I was devastated. I'd had no clue this was going to happen. A couple of weeks prior to that, my boss, the owner of the company, had said to me that I had stability with the company. On the day of my layoff, he gave me one month's notice and informed me to start looking for other employment. I did so immediately, searching on the Internet and through my local newspaper. I had many interests and opportunities, but the pay would not cut it. I ended up accepting a full-time job in an upscale gym as a personal trainer. This job lasted for less than three months. My new boss and I simply did not get along. I didn't know how I was going to make it, but I found a way and managed. I sought guidance from above on what to do and asked for someone to please help me.

My first personal unexplained, divine experience happened during this time. It was the second year I lived in my townhome. I had already lived with my parents for five years before I moved there.

On December 31, 2007, New Year's Eve day, I woke up feeling angelic. I decided to wear a beautiful white blouse with a pair of jeans. My son Jeff and daughter, Kelly, were with me at the time. We had plans to go to my sister's house that evening to celebrate New Year's Eve. Most years I stayed home. I also had been invited to another party, which I declined because I wanted to be around family. The thing was that I felt tired this day and debated whether I should even go to my sister's. The kids wanted to spend time with friends; for whatever reason, I allowed them to.

On my way to drop Jeff off to meet his friend, we stopped briefly at a convenience store so Jeff could get an energy drink. We were in and out quickly and off to McDonald's, where we were meeting Jeff's friend's parents. On my way back home, I followed the same route. As I passed the convenience store, I noticed two cop cars there. Something had just happened, and I felt very lucky that we had missed this altercation. Something inside of me felt divine guidance, as if angels were protecting us. I decided at this point that I would stay home and not go to my sister's for the New Year's celebration.

When I got home, I walked into my house and decided to cook a tray of chicken. My usual way of doing this was in a lasagna pan lined with aluminum foil; I would lay the chicken on top and spice it to my desire. Then in the oven my chicken would go, set for 300° for 45 minutes. It was 6:00 p.m. when I started cooking it. While I waited for chicken to bake, I went upstairs to check my e-mails and play around on the Internet. Then I turned the computer off and journaled about my day. I dozed off and woke up later at 10:00 p.m. I wondered about the time.

I walked downstairs, went into my kitchen, and was caught off guard. I had forgotten I had chicken cooking in the oven. I saw my chicken sitting in the middle of my island, ready to eat. I didn't know what to think. I looked, my mouth ajar and my eyes in wonderment. *What happened?* I thought. *I am the only one here.* My house was locked, the kids were gone, and no one lived with me. *Is this a sign? Of course it is, Barbara,* I told myself. *Angel was here, nonphysical was here, helped me, saved me, turned off my stove, took the chicken out of my oven, and placed it on my island.* I knew divine work was at play. There was no other explanation! I definitely didn't sleepwalk. Also, whenever I baked chicken, when it was finished, I always put it on top of the stove, never on the island.

Also, that Christmas one of my sisters had knitted washcloths and given them as gifts to all of her sisters. She had given me three different colors: white, blue, and teal. I hadn't used any of them yet. For me, since they were not yet used, they were pure. All three had been sitting on my kitchen table, one on top of the other. On this night, I noticed two of them were on the kitchen island, formed like a teepee. I covered the chicken with aluminum foil and went to put it in the refrigerator. When I lifted the pan up, there was the white washcloth, centered under the pan.

I cried in humble thankfulness. I spoke out loud a huge thank you to whomever had come there that night to save me. All day long I had felt angelic, and all day long I had felt like I was being protected, and there I was in the midst of such divine protection. Who was watching out for me? I knew then that I still had a purpose and that I was not going to give up. I didn't.

Meeting Divine in Sleep

The evening of November 12, 2011, I went somewhere into another dimension and had conversation with a higher being. The events earlier that day and the previous day I firmly believe led up to this experience. So I will backtrack to explain.

Late at night on November 10, 2011, a day of being on my moon (menstruation), I was playing my drum. I was tired, but nonetheless I wanted and needed to play. As I fell between a conscious and subconscious state, I was not only aware of the sound of my drum, but I also heard sounds of other instruments playing with me. Even though I felt it lasted only a few seconds, the music I heard playing along with me was the most beautiful music I had ever heard. I had read of experiences similar to mine where one can be in another dimension, experiencing other places and other beings, hearing music from a higher realm, so it was all very magical to me.

I started questioning myself: Was I there? Was I somewhere else? Did someone else come be with me to play with me? Then I said to myself, "Yes, there was!" Yes, I was with someone, and someone was with me, playing music. When something so real and magical happens to you, there are no words in the English language to describe what you see, feel, and know. Words like *joy*, *beauty*, *peace*, and *magic* are the closest words I and others who have had these kind of dimensional experiences can come up with.

But what is beauty to you? How do you feel beauty? When you see the most gorgeous sunrise or sunset, what do you see? What do you feel? These beautiful feelings you see and feel, do they warm your heart? Do they give you a sense of serenity? Do they give you an awareness about them? Is it godly? Is it divine? All of the feelings you feel and see are there inside of you, your spirit, for our spirit connects with the natural beauties of our Earth and universe. Now imagine for a moment feeling all of these things inside of you, and then just go wherever you want, such as another country, another state, another planet. Or go ahead and pick a star and then go another step further into the next dimension. Now you are out in space, a space where there is no distance between where your body is and where your spirit is. And then, right then, you are welcomed by the presence of an enlightened being, and he's talking with you, teaching you things. The two of you communicate back and forth with questions and answers. You know that you are loved always and unconditionally.

Even though I have here with me on Earth an angel in human form, loving me and teaching me truth, this is what I experienced the night on November 12, 2011. It felt like it lasted all night long. I can remember the event, how we met, where we sat, but I do not remember all the words we spoke. As soon as I was out of my body, I could feel that I was a long way away from this planet Earth. I was all spirit, feeling me, knowing who I was, feeling my thoughts, my wishes, and desires for more of this. We both knew of this meeting. I knew him. He knew me. We were expecting each other and this meeting. As I walked closer to him, we embraced, and I immediately spoke personal information to him. I did not have to explain myself. He knew precisely what I meant.

We walked over to a set of chairs next to a small square table. Both the chairs and table were made of silver. The chairs looked to me like folding chairs. I sat in one, and he sat across from me. We were slightly angled toward the table and each other. He talked, and I listened. I was allowed to ask questions, so I did, and he answered every one of them. I remember thinking and wishing that I had a tape recorder so I could go back and relisten to our conversation. As soon as I said that, actually thought it in my mind, he telepathically answered my question. He said, *It is not necessary for you to remember all.* He said the important thing was for me to remember that I had this meeting. The knowing of this meeting.

So yes, I definitely remember the meeting between the two of us. I remember asking one particular question, and he answered, but I do not recall the answer. I asked, "What does 110 mean?" The number 110 represented something. Somehow the subject of sexual abuse was in our conversation as well.

As I gently came back to my body, I awoke just enough to see the time on my clock. It was 5:46 a.m.

Half Empty

It was June 11, 2010, when I settled on the ownership of first my home. What a beautiful day. I almost couldn't believe what I was embarking upon. Me, Barbara Anne Rose, was on my way to the lawyer's office to sign all the papers for my new home. This was one of the big dreams I'd had since separating from my husband.

I remember I couldn't wait to be successful: successful in having my own business and successful in owning my own home because of the financial success of my business. I was already successful in my mind, which had seen me there in the first place. Each step along the way was worth it. To see myself now, hear myself now, and know myself now is all so unreal at times. I went through a lot. I experienced a lot.

Some of what I have experienced may not even seem so much to others, for it wasn't like I experienced far-off, distant lands in travel or food or so-called good times, but I believe I have experienced life. A lot of good and a lot of not so good. I have experienced being with my family, and I've experienced being torn away from my family. I have experienced not being believed by my own family, and I have experienced being believed by my family. I have experienced life as all empty, looking at the glass as half empty, and I have experienced my life as full and seeing my glass as half full. The following story is about how I came to see my glass as half empty or full. It happened when I was in ninth grade.

I remember in ninth grade during a class, my teacher asked us, "How do you see your life? Do you see it as half full or half empty?" We each had a glass filled halfway with water. My teacher asked, "The water in the glass, is it half full or half empty?" I remember thinking, *How do I answer this question? Is this a trick question?* My answer at the time was that it was half empty. I learned that day that if we believed the glass was half empty, we viewed our life negatively, and if we saw the glass as half full, we viewed our life positively.

I didn't like that I viewed my life as half empty, and I blamed this on my family. That was how I had been taught. There was lots of negative in our household. I do not remember much praise, praise with real meaning and real emotion behind it. I really don't think my mom ever meant to cause negative views of men or life in me or my brothers or sisters. She didn't mean to. I know that now. But my living conditions were negative growing up as a child. My life was surrounded by negative. I'd say I was swimming in it, because we—at least I, as I can only speak for myself— saw, heard, and experienced negative, hurtful, harmful behavior. The way my father would speak to my mom and the way he hurt my mom, brothers, and sisters was more painful than anything he ever did to me.

I hated him for hurting my baby sister and the sister who was four years older than me. My older sister was so vulnerable because of her condition, the syndrome she had. She wasn't able to control when she laughed or cried. She wasn't able to control when she became excited. She didn't know how to talk. She would make noises, and through her noises you could tell what her emotions were. When she was excited and happy, she would squeal with delight. It was loud, but it was oh so good to hear. She did require more work because of her condition; not only could she not talk, but she couldn't dress herself. She couldn't brush her teeth. She couldn't take herself to the bathroom or clean herself.

My two older sisters pitched in when they were old enough, and then my younger sister and I helped when we were old enough. For a few years she was in the Special Olympics. A couple of the years I was in high school,

I was her coach. She was good at running, so my mom entered her in running races. This was in 1981 and 1982. One evening this older sister was squealing with delight. Everyone was in bed, wanting to fall asleep, but none of us could sleep because my sister was squealing loudly. I lay in bed on my back, and I heard my father walk out of his bedroom, go into my sister's room, and slap her around to shut her up. *Slap, slap, slap*, he went, and I heard her fall to the ground. Then I heard her crying in pain and sadness. I cried. I was hurt and angry at my father for hurting her so. All I wanted to do was hurt him back.

I forget about some of those times. It's like another life, so very distant from where I am now. So unreal and unbelievable. I am happy and sad and blessed all at the same time. Do we all forget moments in our lives? Do you sometimes forget the good times and seemingly only remember bad or difficult times? If so, why is that? Why? Why? Why? It might be interesting to find out the answer to the *why* question we have in our minds, whether it is in our past, our present, or our future.

But for us to truly be able to love others and ourselves, the only thing we really can do is be ourselves right now, in this moment. We must do what we need to do to serve others. In our service to others, we are in essence also serving ourselves because of the simple joy that giving to others gives us. Gifts of our love, gifts of our thankfulness, gifts of gratitude— these are all priceless. *To be, to live, to breathe life,* our life, the Creator's life, a life that consists of this entire universe. It is so huge that there is no limit. How many people actually do this? How many people actually are this? So many of us live in the hassles of daily life. We get in arguments over small stuff that is quite meaningless. Hear me, see me, need me, want me, love me, help me, save me, etc.

It wasn't until many years later that I started to learn to view my life as half full. It took hard times and some trauma to my mind before I looked at what I had good in my life, and this was my children. A dear friend of mine consistently told me to stay focused on the children, to love them when I was with them. It was difficult at times when going to court over them. I was so scared my husband really would take them away from me for good. I thought how incredibly mean that was to do to me, his children's mother. *Does he hate me that much? Am I that unworthy of receiving love? Am I that messed up?* These were some of the thoughts and fears I had. I knew I had made mistakes, but I knew I was a good mom and loved all of my children more than anyone could ever know. I would lay my life down for them. For my husband to question that hurt! *Have I been that brainwashed by him for me to think I am unworthy?* I had to fight and say, "*No!*" I worked my butt off to prove to everyone that *I was able!* That I was capable. I had to go inside my mind and remind myself that I had been going to the domestic violence shelter for over a year. I had to remind myself that my husband threw things at me, punched holes in walls, threatened violence, burned my clothes, fixed the car so I couldn't drive it. I had to remember all of this in order to help myself, in order to keep my sanity.

Truth, Honor, Beloved

Do you know your truth? Do you know what truth *is*? Is truth just not a lie? No, it is not, because we have been handed down so many perceptions and beliefs from friends, family, religion, society, and government about what they think truth is for us, the truth they want us to follow.

What is truth to one man can be a lie to another.

Truth, ultimate truth, is divine truth. We are all born with it; it is inside us the moment conception takes place. Remember earlier when I mentioned our white light? Our white light is our spirit, and our spirit is all truth. It holds all truth and knows all truth. Our spirit is one with our Creator. Since we are one with creation, our spirit knows truths. There is no separation. We have our individuality, as does all else, but we are all one with our spirit and the spirit world. This happens on a micro cosmic level and on a macro cosmic level. I reference micro cosmic meaning within the physical world of ourselves-our body and our world, within our relations with others, with society and on this planet called Earth. I refer macro cosmic as spiritually in the spirit world-the unseen world. Let me help you understand more when I use the word spirit as I have used and continue to use in this book. Sometimes in my writing I use the word spirit as The Spirit within you, meaning one, micro cosmically. Your one spirit of white light within you associating with the spirit of white light in others. Sometimes I use the word Spirit when describing all spirits. It is not ***the spirit*** as in one spirit but it ***is spirit***; which encompasses all spirits. The letter "s" turning the word spirit into spirits isn't always necessary when writing about spirit because spirit is a wide vast word encompassing ***all*** of spirit. Can you understand? When I say "our spirit" it represents our spirit within. When I say "spirit" it may represent one nonphysical spirit, or many, or even all of the spirits in the spirit world. So use of the word "the" in front of the word "spirit" is not necessary when writing about spirit world/spirits in the spirit world and or other dimensions because the use of the word "the" has a perception to the mind as a meaning of "one." For instance: Sally walked into the sewing room to get **the** measuring tape for her mom. Or: Tom found **the** book he wanted in the library. Another example that may better help your understanding is the word "deer" or "fish." Those two words when describing deer or fish can be meant singular or plural. Now, do you understand when I use the word "spirit" as one or more than one when talking about spirit on a macro cosmic level?

The trouble is that we are not all connected to our spirit. If we don't feel that connection, we feel separate, so we think and act as if we are separate from it. And if we're feeling separate, thinking and acting separate from our spirit, then we have a hard time connecting, thriving, and growing with one another. Once we take notice that we even have a spirit, the white light in each of us, we can then begin to take notice of and listen to our minds and bodies.

If the spirit knows all truth and you are disconnected from your spirit, how do you go about being connected again? Ask. Simply ask yourself to be reconnected, and the spirit will give you an answer, one you will be able to understand. It will come to you in terms you can relate to and in a way that gets your attention. For example, let's say you enjoy reading; your answer may come to you through a book, newspaper, or magazine. It may not necessarily be the book itself, but something in your mind that becomes aware of something bigger, talks to you, connects with you. Follow this inner prompting.

Or if you enjoy a certain sport, let's say an outdoor sport, the answer might come to you through nature, through the wind or the birds that fly through the air, fly past your face, or perch close to you. Or you may hear someone say something that happened to get your attention. If you are inside a building, the spirit may get your attention again through something someone else says that you overhear. Pay attention to all around you. Yes, even to children. They are wiser than you realize. Pay attention to the scoreboard. A number or group of numbers might speak to you. It could be a bird that caught your eye or maybe even a cat or dog that you noticed slip into a building. Colors, a diagram layout on the basketball, volleyball, or soccer courts. Pay attention to all of these things. A feeling, thought, or vision might flash across your mind like a picture on a movie screen or the flash of a camera, and you might wonder, *What was that? That was a weird thought.* Even smells may prompt a thought, emotion, or memory to help give you an answer upon which to contemplate.

Answers can come from anywhere and everywhere, from anyone, or from anything. Keep your senses open. As long as you keep an open mind, the truth will come in a way you will recognize. Once you can open your mind or your heart, whichever is easier for you to open first, and keep it open, once you start opening your heart or mind and feel good about yourself, then you should start working on another sense, then another, and then another until you can feel, see, hear, taste, smell, and know all more fully.

It is all good once you start awakening to the divine. Then you can have fun with it for a while. Test yourself with some easy questions and work on going deeper, asking more compelling questions. Ask questions about other people to get a sense of the energy between the two of you. As you practice and become consistent, you will find yourself getting better and better. But make sure you always ask to know truths. Ask from a loving state, not from a state of selfishness. Allow your curiosity to come from a loving state.

Remember, love leads to more love. More love brings more light. Light feeds light, and love feeds love. Ask and it is given. Be humble about it and accept the answers that come your way with thankfulness. If the answer doesn't feel good, it's still an answer, and the answer is always right when it comes from your spirit. Remember, your spirit knows all truth, and sometimes the truth is troubling. We must embrace this and keep asking questions.

Part of the truthful divine is in honor. The lack of honoring ourselves and the lack of honoring each other does not come from the divine. The word *honor* comes from honesty, and to be honest with ourselves and one another, we must be able to openly recognize each other. Jumping out or away from any relationship without showing honor to oneself and the other person involved does neither any good. Quite the contrary, it can make the situation worse.

I suggest choosing your actions and reactions very carefully. No one is right, and no one is wrong. We tend to think, *I am right and you are wrong*, but an attitude like that only causes a back-and-forth exchange of words. Each person needs to accept and take responsibility for his or her own self. If someone leaves for whatever reason, it's on him or her, not you. So please, do yourself a favor and love you no matter what. There is nothing you can physically do or say to make things right or better. All you can really do is send loving energy, being careful not to condemn the other person in your mind or thoughts, because thought is an energy that travels. Anything done or said out of fear is not going in the upward, forward direction.

I am not saying you don't have a right to speak your feelings. I just want you to consider where they are coming from. Do these feelings and emotions come from a source of fear or anger? I know it is difficult sometimes to not quite know what to do or say. This is not just a woman thing. This is a human thing. I particularly do not like or care for the separation of man and woman, like we are two completely different entities. We're all human. We all have thoughts, fears, emotions, desires, needs, and wants we would like to express to our partner and feel safe doing it.

Let's get past the male/female victim roles that suggest we have to act a certain way to catch and keep him or her. Just be yourself. It appears to me that everyone has drifted away from his or her true self. We become selfish, egotistical, and arrogant in our ways and forget we are human beings. We become desensitized and do not take into consideration how others feel. We don't consider how others may feel if we say or do things that could possibly jeopardize our relationships.

I know that we all have pasts and that we all want and need to be loved and cared for, but we end up doing it in such a backward way. We have a tendency to place blame on everyone or everything else around us and outside of us instead of working from our own source within. Remember the flower in the preface of this book? The flowers that we all are? Our spirit resides in the center of our solar plexus; where all love resides.

We each come into this world with one body, and we die, leaving this one body behind. Let's all wake up and smell the roses. Hold on and see all the goodness you are and don't take anyone or anything for granted. Life is a gift. You are a gift.

There are many gifts in you to use to express and give joy to other people and to yourself. Many people know and realize that life is a gift, but how many of us actually treat all human beings in such a way? We have a tendency to make automatic decisions about what we think another person is, based simply on what we see at face value. We make automatic decisions about other people based on the color of their skin. We make automatic decisions about other people because of which church they belong to. We make automatic decisions about other people because they speak different languages. We make automatic decisions about other people because of their sexual orientation. It is time for us to get out of ourselves so that we can get back inside of ourselves, back inside to our spirit.

This world focuses too much on the physical body, on materialistic things, on any outside source we think can help us when in fact we are the only ones who can help us. We help ourselves by making the intention to go inside to our spirit, where all love and truth resides. Jesus has taught that we are all one and the truth resides within us, not a church, not a building, not a book. Even though I may insert some truth teachings into this book, it is merely information for you to consider. Take the information inside of you and honestly look at it. This book I write is not a book on truth teachings; rather, it is a book to help inspire you to open your mind and spirit to the truth that is already inside of your spirit, your white light.

This white light, our spirit we have within our bodies is a beloved, honorable and cherished entity of purity. To be beloveds, to love, honor and cherish it is a must we be the beloved to ourselves first. We must love us first. We must honor ourselves first. We must cherish ourselves first. It is required we be these things for ourselves before we can truly give in these ways to others. I love me. I love you. Love me, my beloved, my high priestess, God, goddess. Honor yourself. Honor me. Honor us. I honor you. I honor me. I honor us. What ever happened to honor? It seems lost.

Is it lost? What does it mean? What exactly does it mean? What does it feel like? We need to feel more. We need to feel with our hearts' deep soul longings. Is there anyone out there? Am I the only one? Are you the only one? We need to touch each other again. We need to love each other again. We need to embrace each other again. It has been lost. We need peace again!

Do you believe that we *can* have peace again? Not peace just as in a lack of war. Peace among all people. Peace in our minds, our hearts, and our spirits. We must have peace within ourselves first. We cannot teach peace. We cannot teach love. We cannot teach joy. We must live all of these things inside of us all of the time. We teach by being these things. If you want peace, then *be* peace. If you want joy, then *be* joy. If you want love, then *be* love. Everything always starts and ends with you. You and only you. There is really no other way around it.

Truth resides in us all, all of the time. We are confused and backward when we continually seek all these things—truth, peace, joy, etc.— from outside sources. Sure, it is okay to have a little help and guidance along the way, but ultimately it is you within you. Stop fighting against yourself. When we run away, we are not running from a place or person or circumstance. We are really running from ourselves. Some people run for their entire lives. The thing is, you take it with you into your next life. How long must you continue to run? How low will you go?

Stop this madness of your own creation. It's your job to create your own life and no one else's. So create your own life. We each have dreams. We each have goals. We each have desires. Use them to inspire you. As you do this, not only are you giving yourself your own inspiration, but you inspire others around you. You ignite a fire within you for others to see and feel. People will feel you. People will see you. People will become aware of all of who you are when you tap into your own divine self. People will be drawn to you, wanting and craving to be in your presence. What a precious gift this is. A gift that is so spiritually strong and powerful that no amount of money can ever buy it. And this is all because of your own desire and the work you do when you go inside yourself to bring forth your own dreams! I want you to never ever stop dreaming. I dare you to dream big!

Divinity is in love, in honor, in faith, and in truth. It is our spiritual duty to not place judgment on anyone. Demands and authority statements like, "You can't do that anymore" make people feel like their free will has been taken away. Husbands want to control their wives, and wives want to control their husbands. This is why people leave. Men need love and touch from women. Women want to know their men are theirs and only theirs.

People are afraid to share. In all honesty, we really do not belong to anyone, for we belong to our spirit and our Creator because our Creator is the one who gave us this life, not man. It is our spiritual duty at all times to love and forgive others. We do not know when someone is a good person; neither do we know when someone is a bad person. There are times we all do good things, and there are times we all do bad things, but we are not here to cast judgment on whether this person is good or bad.

We judge not only when we label someone as bad but also when we label someone as good, for we do not know the minds and hearts of those around us or even those in our home. We don't know their pasts, how they grew up, how they were treated in their childhoods. There could be a zillion reasons why people do what they do. You may find someone who claims he or she doesn't judge, but when it gets down to the nitty-gritty, you will typically find that he or she does. We judge more often than we realize.

The same holds true when an individual claims he or she has no worry, fear, or doubt. Once you start asking questions, you will see that there are worries, fears, and doubts living within his or her body. If we truly had no worry, fear, or doubt, then we would be fearless. But the world in which we live is built upon fear. It preys upon us, wanting us to have fear so that we play into this game of control and greed. It's a good cop/bad cop game. We need to watch ourselves with caution; we need to pay attention to our actions and reactions and the actions and reactions of the people around us. In time, people present their own truths of who they are. In time, the truth will always come forward.

It is a shame that people seek to control others in whatever form they see fit in order to meet their own selfish desires of the flesh. Divine love must start within, and we can only have divine love with another person when he or she has divine love within him or herself. When we have divine love, when we *are* divine love in this state, we are then truly free.

We lie to ourselves because we are too afraid to know the truth, so we hide from it as long as we can. We bury it deep and keep it there for so long that we do not even know who we are anymore. We do not know who anyone else is anymore. We turn into flesh predators eating away the spirit of others. Once we recognize this truth, we can then start to deal with our own selves. The power is always within you and never another. Each one of us has our own power. This power is our light spirit within.

My love, my beloved, my divine being, my fellow baby child of our Creator, crawl with me, walk with me, let me help you, let me show you the way. I do my best here to help you understand that I am not any different than you. I may be further along than many, but I am still a baby child spiritually. We're all grown men and women with baby spirits searching for truth, searching for real love and guidance. Our spirit seeks to truly have faith and surrender to the divine, our supreme Creator, the ceaselessly and seamlessly amazing brilliant white light, this Creator we may one day meet after the passing of our bodies. When this happens, we will have an infinite supply of beauty and boundless gifts of love.

I recommend for you to say to yourself some of the following affirmations. They may help you in your journey. Repeating them over and over again in your mind and out loud is a powerful tool to use in helping yourself to love you more fully.

- I am a beautiful man.
- I am a beautiful woman.
- I am a mighty power force of white light.
- I am free.
- I am peace.
- I am joy.
- I am merciful.
- I am humbly grateful.
- I am a being of light and love, expecting nothing, thankful for everything, and I do not set hopes or expectations in front of me. I love the life in front of me today with all the love that comes from within my heart.

Love is divine. Divine is love. There is only one love, and that is divine love. Love is a word many people use loosely, thinking they know what it means. Do you not see or know the true meaning of love? This world in which we live is a world of hate, which creates control. If this world were in fact a world of love, we would not be where we are right now. There would be no jails, no penitentiaries, no judge condemning someone as guilty. We would not have poverty or discord with other countries. We would not have ill feelings toward another ... ever. Jesus taught us to love unconditionally. We would all hold hands and in unison thank our Creator and all the angels from a state of gratitude.

When we love and forgive, we are not accepting the bad caused by another person. We love sometimes by letting go, getting that person's circle of life out of ours. We love us and them enough to release them from us and allow the Creator to do the work. If we allow ourselves to have ill thoughts toward someone else, we are essentially playing the judge. For instance, if I still held anger toward my father or ex-husband, I would be doing myself harm, creating bad vibrations toward me and back around into my life like a boomerang.

What you give out, you will always get back. It is our circle of life. Take some time to think more on this. I want you to think big, think small, and go back into your life as far as you can remember. As you think about this, what age are you? What memory pops into your head? Where are you? Who were you with? If you are with anyone, is it a friend? A parent? A family member? A pet? A teacher? Can you hear words being said to you in this memory? Can you see around you, your surroundings? Are you picking up on any smells?

Take a moment now and close your eyes. Take five to ten slow, deep breaths in and out through your nose. Do not breathe out of your mouth, for you will expel this energy out of your body. I want you to feel inside your body. I want you to feel the you in you. With each breath in and out through your nose, take this breath of life down deeper into yourself. Down from one level to another and to another. Don't be hard on yourself if at first you don't succeed.

I want you to practice this exercise daily, maybe even several times a day. As you do this, have a picture in your mind of what love looks like to you. Once you can see this picture in your mind's eye, go into how this picture feels. I want you to feel, feel, feel and soak, soak, soak all of this in. I want you to be in a state of letting yourself go. I want you to feel your body. I want you to be aware of any tension in your body. Are any certain parts of your body feeling more tense than others? Is your neck more stiff than your legs? Are you holding tension in your feet? Are you holding tension in your hands? People typically hold tension in their shoulders, neck, or any place in their backs, but we forget we can hold tension in any muscle. Do you hold tension in your right pinky toe? Do we stop to make ourselves aware of this?

In order for us to feel tension in other parts of our bodies, we need to teach ourselves to be more aware. We forget the small things that our bodies speak to us. It is not until our bodies are sometimes to the point of breaking us down that we start to become more aware of how we work. Of how our bodies speak to us. Of how our spirit speaks to us. The spirit is always speaking to us, but are we listening? Or do we only start to listen once we are diagnosed with cancer, diabetes, fibromyalgia, or any other debilitating disease?

It seems we are constantly traveling at such a fast pace that we become walking zombies, just doing what we need to do to pay bills. We have to do this, and we have to do that. We can still take care of all of our worldly responsibilities *and* take a few moments out of our days to breathe and go within. The more you are consciously aware of your breathing, the more you will want to be aware. You say you don't have time? You don't have time to breathe?

You are worth taking the time to stop and breathe and find your life. If you are living in a crazy world, it is a crazy world you have helped create. You are the only one who has the power to change negatives into positives, the cup from half empty to half full. You can choose your life, and you can choose your death. You have the power of free will to do better for yourself. We all can do better for ourselves. If we think we have reached our heights in growth and learning, then we say to ourselves, "I don't need to grow anymore. I know all I need to know. I am just fine." But there is always room for growth, no matter how enlightened or spiritual we claim to be. Ego is a huge force that allows us to stop in this growth.

Go down inside of yourself. Breathe in through your nose and out through your nose. Then you can learn to feel more of who you are. You can reach down deeper into your spirit. You can find the answer(s) you have been seeking for years. Some people search and search all of their lives and never find their answers. Most likely the reason is because they are searching outside themselves. They look to doctors, thinking they know all the answers, like doctors are some gods. We look for quick fixes. Why do you think there are so many drugs out there? Take this pill so you can lose weight. Take this pill so your heart rate will go back to normal.

It is time for all of us to search within for all of our answers, for us to be guided by spirit. It is up to us to desire this so badly that we will take a few moments of every day to go within. We need to care about us enough to do the work. The more consistent we become, the easier it becomes, and the easier it becomes, the more we open ourselves to feel, to be. When we are directed by our spirit, we are happy because only love lives there. Changes can be subtle, and that's a good thing. It's okay. Weeks, maybe months will go by, and you will stop to think, *Wow, I can't believe I used to do that* or *Wow, I can't believe I used to think that way. This makes so much more sense to me. Thank you.*

When this happens, it is okay to thank me, but what I would rather you do is thank yourself. Thank yourself for saying yes to you. Thank yourself for keeping at it, for being committed to yourself, because you are important and you are worth it. You will love yourself for it. You will see more, hear more, know more, and feel more. You will *be* more of who you really are. I also would like you to be aware of your dreams. You may find that they change. You may find them to be more detailed. You may feel like you're dreaming but also in a different state of subconsciousness. Say, maybe it's a dream within a dream or in more than one dimension!

When you do your breathing exercises, find a spot out of the way from everyone else. You will need to create your own special place, such as your bedroom, a sunroom, or reading area. Find a cozy place you can throw an area rug down, sit in the middle of it, and set candles around you to give off light. If you wish, play long, gentle music in the background to help guide you inside. Music specifically made for brainwave action, such as theta healing vibrational music, might be particularly helpful. For some people, no background music works better. They like the silence or hearing sounds of nature. I personally like either silence or my vibrational sound healing CD.

Even though the first three sentences in the following exercise are the same they are meant to be the same to help you *feel* the words you are about to read. To say powerful words over and over again speaks to your mind truth. As you are willing and surrender to these words they *will* fill your mind, body and emotions so your spirit *can* rule your mind, body and emotions.

- My spirit rules my mind, my body, and my emotions.
- My spirit rules my mind, my body, and my emotions.
- My spirit rules my mind, my body, and my emotions.
- I am strong. I claim my strength. I claim my power.
- I claim my spiritual power.

I believe the following words given to me from my Angel Bearer of Light are important to insert here so please think on them:

> *Power is not to be used from our egos, as most tend to do. The word power is misunderstood because the ego wants to be noted as powerful. Spiritual power is pure energy of love, creation energy seen as the white light, the Creator's light within us.*

There may be times we find it difficult to get through emotions we have, especially when these emotions are hindering us, getting in the way of us doing what we know we should do. It is the emotion of fear that we need to break through. We need to recognize them when they appear and not be ruled by them. When we are ruled by our own emotions, we are taking away our own spiritual power. We settle for less than what we know we deserve. We fight for what we think we should rightly have, fighting with anger. We start to think it is our right to fight back with a vengeance. It is like a war, back and forth with an opposing victim. Yet who is the one really playing victim in this war? Is it them? Is it you? Is it both sides? In any war, we sit ourselves in a front-seat view of hell. War has no place in our spiritual enlightenment. Fear has no place in our spiritual enlightenment. If at any time you become afraid, just forgive yourself. We have many fears. Many are raised in fear. So many doubts we have are about us or others or life itself. Who put these fears inside us? Where do they come from? Why are they there to begin with anyway? I wish for everyone that not one of us has any fear, but we do. They are there. Let's take responsibility of these fears we have. Let's recognize that we have them and work through them one by one, pushing ourselves through to the truth. To feel them, to know that they are there. We need to deal with our fears using our spirit. As we open ourselves to feel spirit within us, we can get through anything. We need to feel, move out of ourselves, love ourselves, love others, accept where we are right now on any given day and moment. We are born perfect, but through our upbringings with parents or friends or family, along with our own mess-ups we have created, we can begin to become free from them.

In the week of November 5, 2011, I caught myself feeling sad and lonely and missing certain loved ones, but I knew I must pick myself up out of these negative emotions and feelings. I was the only one who could do that. We all have moments when we wish such and such a person would come by and save us, or we wonder in our minds or maybe even say out loud to our God, "Why am I still alone? Why am I still single? Why hasn't he or she come back?" We think of this and that, sometimes over and over and over again, so much so that we drive ourselves crazy. If anyone is around us, we may drive these other people crazy too, for we can only continue acting this way for so long before we push people away. We push our own selves away. We push our spirit selves down, not allowing the love our spirit has to heal ourselves. The spirit within loves us and is there for us to use. To use for our own good. Let yourself meet you. You will be in awe when you first meet and recognize yourself.

I remember a significant time like this. It was at the end of 2010. It happened during a time when I was writing an e-mail to a beloved. I felt the physical me meet the light spirit within me. I felt it with such intensity that I could not help but shed tears of gratefulness. I had finally met myself, the physical with the divine. I felt this just as if you and I were sitting across the table from one another. Imagine sitting across the table from your best friend or your mom or dad or anyone with whom you have a close, heart-to-heart connection. Now see them in your mind, you and the one you're closely connected to, looking directly into each other's eyes. See his or her eyes. Look deeply into this person's eyes and reach down inside his or her spirit. Stay in this moment for a time. Get used to feeling this, embracing it. Know how powerful the love you are feeling is. Practice doing this exercise for a time, maybe a week or maybe a month or two, before you attempt to imagine meeting yourself. It is easier to imagine a loved one first before visiting ourselves.

When you want to visit yourself, you may want to practice it in front of a mirror so you have your own face, your own eyes to look into. Stay in front of the mirror for at least five minutes. If you feel unable to look at yourself for this amount of time, look away and then look right back at yourself quickly. You may find it easy. You may find it difficult. That depends on how much healing needs to take place within you. Don't give up. Stay committed to yourself and do this every day for at least five minutes. Commit yourself to the exercise.

This is the beginning. You might feel pain that is there. Keep your eyes on your eyes in the mirror during any pain that shows itself. Let the feelings move through you and out of you. Recognize that it is okay that these feelings are here for you to feel and recognize. If you need to cry, then cry. If you need to scream, then scream. If you want to laugh, then laugh. This is part of the process of you learning to see you and love all of you so that you can reach a point where you can forgive all of you.

May I suggest you have some paper and a pen next to you to write everything down that you see and feel? Keep a diary. You may want to label it *mirror diary*. I recommend that the best time to do this exercise is before you lay down to bed. I recommend doing it before bed so that if pain or fear of any kind comes up, you are not around the public. You will have time to sleep on it. As you fall asleep, say to yourself the following:

- I am peace.
- I am love.
- I am joy.
- I am divine.
- I am beautiful.

Fall asleep speaking these words over and over and over again. Say them even if you don't believe them … yet. Speak positively to yourself. The more you speak positively to yourself, even if it feels foreign to you, the more you will eventually begin to believe these things are true, because your spirit is all of these things. Only good resides here. You are the one who makes the first step. This is your choice. This is your free will.

When I was feeling sad and down the week of November fifth, I took notice of it and took an important step, asking myself where these feelings were coming from. I knew it was not good or in the best interests of my spirit to feel such a way, because I knew I had much to be thankful for. I thought first before voicing any negative thought because I knew that voicing negativity would certainly not serve me or the air I breathed around me. I thought about things I was most grateful for and voiced these. I voiced, "I am thankful I have a home for shelter. I am thankful I have two vehicles I can use to travel from one place to another. I am thankful I have my children. I am thankful I have my health. I am thankful I have two arms and two legs that I am able to use. I am thankful I love me. I am thankful for my friends who love me. I am thankful I do the work I do because I know it is important. I am thankful I am protected by my Angel Bearer of Light."

Do you see a pattern of my thankfulness, starting with things that lead to family and friends and then lead to myself and on to higher powers? I said all of this out loud while driving my car. I pushed myself through, making a conscious decision to focus on all positive. I could have easily chosen to cry tears and ask why such and such hadn't happened yet. I could have gone home and fallen asleep on my couch at 2:00 p.m., but I didn't do that. I knew I needed to write. I knew I needed to work from my spirit and allow my spirit to rule my emotions, my mind, and my body. In these moments, I consciously made the decision to choose life! I chose to love and live, not just for me but for every one of you who reads these words.

Anyone of us can get caught up in the woe-is-me syndrome, bowing down to the punisher that hunches over our shoulders, secretly whispering in our ears, "Go ahead. It's okay to whine and cry. I'll be right beside you, and as you sleep I will continue to whisper in your mind things you haven't accomplished, places you haven't gone, so many wants you haven't fulfilled. You fool, why haven't you done it? Yes, bow to me, my friend." All of these statements came from the punisher. I said no to the punisher! I would not bow down to him. I said, "I am strong, and I will write my book! You devil, go away! I will not serve you! I have people to help." Yes, yes, yes, I serve my light! I only serve the powers of light—angels. Angels of Light are on my side, and light will always prevail when I use my own light.

We will be tested. We will be tested to see just how faithful we are to our light. Sometimes these tests may slowly work upon you, softly and subtly. Take notice of everything and everyone around you. Take notice of your own self, your actions and re-actions. Not just of others but of yourself and your state of health.

The week of November 5, 2011, I suffered from seasonal allergies. It started with my throat, which became scratchy and dry, and I had a hard time sleeping at night because of it. I took a lozenge and kept water on my bedside table. My allergies worked themselves up into my nose and then to my eyes and finally to my head, causing a headache. The reading glasses I wore didn't help either. Sometimes they caused headaches too. I felt weak all over. I was even slightly nauseous. I knew my body needed rest. My spirit told me to not work out, so I didn't. I couldn't have even if I tried. It felt like there was a spiritual battle going on inside of me.

Some people think working out through sickness helps. No, my dear ones, it does not. It only places more stress on the body. The body needs less stress to heal itself. On top of that, when you are aware that your body is informing you to take it easy, it is best to listen to it. Listen to what your spirit is saying about how to deal with your body when it is not up to par.

If it tells you to sleep, then sleep. If it tells you to close your eyes, even if only for five minutes, do it. You'll thank yourself.

I learned through all that my Angel Bearer of Light speaks that spirits don't get bigger or wider or smaller or brighter. It is our minds that perceive our spirit as doing so. Truth does not "come" to us. The truth is never hidden. All of the truth is out there once we get in right frame of spirit. Then we can see it and pick it like a plump cherry. We are all aware that we do not use all of our brain. We use about 10 percent of it. Once we open ourselves to want to be more aware of all things, the brains we have are a doorway to receive much more information. When we open our spirit to receive truths with our open brains, the truth shows itself; therefore, you can see it, know it, and feel it in order for you to use it for yourself. Our mind has the capacity to view life circumstances from the light or the dark side. Choose light!

During these few days, my mind and spirit were so open to receiving information, my body felt like a sponge so saturated with information that I couldn't go anywhere or function at top level. I was physically tired and needed to take it gently and easily. I was like a baby learning how to walk or talk, stumbling over words, falling down and picking myself back up again. Babies and small children are sponges, picking up information from all over the place. They learn, touch, feel, eat, suck, hear. They scoot, crawl, roll over, sit up, stand up, fall down, walk a step or two, plop down on their cute little behinds, and then work on getting back up to walk again.

We too are babies. We are spiritual babies learning spiritual truths. In order for our minds to see these truths, we need to open ourselves to receive them. We need to realize all the misbeliefs we have grown up with so that we can open. Currently we are either open or closed. When we are open, we have willing hearts to listen and consider what is being said.

You may ask yourself, "Why should I listen to you?" Well, the truth is you don't have to listen to me because you have free will. You might want to at least consider allowing your soul to listen. My Angel Bearer of Light guides me and teaches me universal truths. You can choose to believe in angels or you can choose not to. I cannot and will not force anything upon you. You decided to purchase this book and read it for a reason. Something inside you reached out and caused you to pick it up, open it to a page, and read a passage, or maybe you read something on the front or back cover that struck your interest and you bought it. Listen to that voice again. Keep opening your mind to learn, understand, and grow.

Of course, there may be moments when you have difficulty comprehending or understanding some things, and that is okay. We're not going to get it every time. The important thing is to keep yourself open. When you continue to do that, you'll have a moment of what feels like *It came to me!* An ah-ha moment. Do you see? It's not that *it* came to you. Your mind was open to receiving the information, and your spirit was in its right frame to receive it. Both need to be in place for you to pick up this information like a plump cherry.

Miracles are only considered miracles in the physical world. In the spirit world, miracles are natural everyday occurrences. It's just energy working at a higher vibration. We have access to this energy of truth at all times, but many people are not aware it is there, and many times—the majority of times—if we do know it is there, we do not know how to fully see it so we can use it properly. We form a veil between us and the truth. The veil was not placed there by someone or something else. We put it there. Since we're the ones who put this veil there, created this veil between us and truth, we are the only ones who can take it down. The more quickly we take it down completely and for good, the more quickly we will see truth.

Why would you not want to take it down? Are you afraid of what the truth holds? Are you worried you will fail at listening or following through because you think it will be hard? I personally would rather know the truth and live my life the best way I knew how than not know truths and take chances. Are you afraid the words spoken to you will hurt because they might be so different than what you have learned growing up? That maybe you have messed up so much in your life so far that you won't feel worthy of doing differently now, so why bother? It is never too late to seek truth or to see more, learn more, love more, and *be* more.

People get offended by words because their minds aren't in the right place. Our thoughts turn to words, which turn to actions. Character is developed by our actions. Actions are thoughts and words acted out. We need to take time to invest in our spirit. Do you realize that we as a people drink our own hate? We all have our own circles of life, and our hate will find us and come back to us with a fierceness if we do not learn more about the spirit we have inside us and use it for our good.

If we humans really want to learn, we must surrender to the divine. We must let go of our egos. There is darkness in ego, and we must not stand for darkness. Seek light. Seek truth. The truth is in the light. The light is within you; therefore, truth is in you. Seek your own light, and it is there that you will see truth.

We have created so many walls of fear that get in our way. We must be the ones to break down these walls. I want you to feel spiritually high all of the time. I want you to be in love with you, the *you* in you. I want you to see you, embrace you, be *you*. When you reach this state of loving and knowing, you will find that there are no words in the English language to express all that you feel. The divine is all divine. It is so big and beautiful that we are not able to grasp the vastness of it all. We are unable to comprehend even a fraction of it, but as we get a glimpse of this fraction, we will be in awe of it. It is a beautiful thing. Because of this, we must be grateful to all spirits of love and light. Use the exercises I have given you in previous chapters. Go through all of the questions I have presented and continue to present them to you and answer them.

Isn't it interesting how some people say they are spiritual; they believe in spiritual things and believe in angels, but when they are presented with a piece of knowledge that is unfamiliar, they question the existence of higher knowings, angels, masters of light, and love? Many don't believe until they see; some sort of physical manifestation must occur in order for them to believe. Their trust and faith is limited to what they already know.

Our limited minds keep us from experiencing more. We seem to have a hard time with faith and trust. The *I* within the word *faith* is us. The *U* within the word *truth* is us. We must take one step at a time, one moment at a time, one lesson at a time, one forgiveness at a time. As I continue my life of learning and growing, loving and forgiving, I see more of where I was, how I acted, and how I reacted to people and events. By no means have I ever thought that I had my life all together. There are things I know and things I do not know. I know much more now than I did even six months ago, and I am happy and grateful for that. I know there will always be more that I want to know, and I will know because of my sincere desire to learn everything my Angel Bearer of Light chooses to teach me.

CHAPTER 16

Praising

I ask you, whom do you praise? How do you praise? Why do you praise? Is it out of selfish needs that want to be met? Does it come from your physical self or your divine self? Let's take a look at each of these questions separately and go deeper, deeper than I believe you may have ever thought before.

Whom Do You Praise?

Is it Jehovah? Is it the Buddha? Is it Krishna? Is it Jesus? Is it one particular person you associate with a religion? Is it an animal?

There are many different religions, and they all claim theirs is the right one. They claim their religion has the almighty truth to all because it's in a book written by man and has been handed down for hundreds or thousands of years. I think almost everyone believes you can't believe everything you read, or everything you see because everyone has their own interpretations of what they read, see, or hear.

We all want to make ourselves the best; we want to sound the best, look the best, be the best. Self-righteousness is what many people mistakenly seek, not self-divinity. We have been misled. Why should you listen to me as you read the words in this book? It is not that I think I know all, but I believe I know enough to offer some form of guidance. Some things I have learned have been given to me from my Angel Bearer of Light. It is real, very real. Angels of Light and love exist here on Earth in human bodies.

To praise with truth, we must first have an open heart. We must have an open mind. We must be willing to go beyond our normal way of thinking. We must learn to become open in order to get past our religious upbringings, if we had any. Some people have no foundation to any truth whatsoever. It is good to open ourselves up to the unknown of the nonphysical world. There lies the mystery. Angels of Light, and only Angels of Light, are mystics. Humans are not. We may be mystical, enjoying mystical things and mystical ideas, but we are mortals, not mystics.

So whom do you praise? I eagerly awaited the answer to this question from my Angel Bearer of Light. He informed me it is our Creator whom we must praise, to whom we must give glory, honor, and gratitude. To be grateful in everything we do. To be grateful in every place we go. To be grateful in all situations. It requires really no effort to be grateful, to show our gratitude.

When you are down and feel as if there is no one in your life who cares, listens, or understands, I want you to know that even though you feel this way, it does not mean you are not loved or cared for. It does not mean that there is nothing in your life worthy of being grateful for. Being alive and breathing is sufficient to be grateful for, for our Creator has given us life. Our Creator blew the breath of life into you when you were born and continues to do so every day you are alive. It is up to you to use this breath of life to its fullest capacity by taking care of your mind, body, and soul. Give breath to your mind. Give breath to your body. Give breath to your soul. Praise and give gratitude every single day that you have this breath of life. Then praise and give gratitude for the body you have that walks, talks, sees, hears, feels, and tastes. It is precious. No possessions, no money, no nothing can purchase the value of life-giving breath.

I have always been one to remind people of simple basic workouts, how to eat, how to be. I did this when I personally trained people and when I helped them learn how to eat better. Simple basics are all we really ever want anyway. We want our life to be easy or easier than what we already have. Simple exercises for the body to keep it in shape. Simple, quick meals to keep our bodies healthy. So it is with our spirit. Just like with an exercise program and diet, it takes commitment and dedication from you. It requires a willing, open heart and mind.

Our Creator creates. Think on that for a while. Our Creator creates. What do you think that means? Think about the male and female body for a moment. Which one creates life? Man cannot create life. They only have the sperm that can enable life to be made. But nothing is born or created without the woman. Women carry, nurture, and grow the child within their bodies. Without woman, there is no creation of following generations. So to praise to a man as Creator is incorrect, for men are unable to create. It is my knowing and the lessons of my Angel Bearer of Light that teach and guide me that say our Creator is female. That women have the authority and spiritual power over men. This does not imply that we as women are higher or above or that we are smarter or wiser or more intelligent. It only means that we are creators, that we create life beings.

We women have a special connection with the Creator because of our wombs and our female parts. We must give honor and praise to the Creator of all life, all things, all animals, all of the stars and the moon and the sun, all plant life. Everything on this Earth in its purest form is here because of our Creator. If you are a man you may be thinking, *I am a man. I create. I create buildings out of brick, stone, and mortar.* This is not what I mean when I say create. That kind of creation is artificial.

There's nothing like our Mother Earth and our Creator. Yes, we are all one. We are all independent from one another, yet we are also intertwined and connected to one another and to all of life because of our Creator. The spirit we have inside us connects us on a macrocosmic and microcosmic level. On this spirit level, we all are just as connected to people who live across the continent as we are to those living in our own towns and houses. It is so big and so small at the same time.

This may be difficult for you to understand or comprehend. I invite you to read this again and allow the words to soak into your being. Allow the words to soak into your body, mind, and soul. As you allow this—and notice how I say, *as you allow*—you will begin to feel more. Your mind will begin to expand as if it is opening space for more information to be understood and sit there in the brain. Let your spirit do the work for you.

The spirit always works for you, for spirit is made of all the colors of the rainbow, forming a brilliant, white light inside of us. Just as spirit always loves you and accepts you, so does our Creator—always there, always loving, always patient, always joyful. You, the human mind and body, is the one required to do the asking. Life begins when you say yes to it. Life begins and ends with you. You either treat your life and the lives around you from your physical, selfish state or through your spiritual, divine state. It cannot be done through both at the same time.

So remember to give thankfulness, to be in gratitude, and to remain in gratitude to the Creator all the time. As you do this, honoring your Creator, you will find that you begin to honor all else.

Why Do You Praise?

Why do you praise? Is it for monetary gain? Is it for a better job? Is it because you want to receive a new love or more love? Why do *you* praise? Ask yourself that question right now. Right now after reading the question, what do you feel? Where in your body do you feel it? What is being spoken to you? Look inside, really close, really deep, to tap into these feelings or sensations. Does it come from below your heart? At your heart? Above your heart? Do you feel it in the pit of your stomach? Is there a choking sensation/feeling in your throat? Be aware of your body. Don't allow your body to take over your own right mind. You can do this because you are a being of white light. There is a spirit of love within you that you can see, feel, hear and know. Trust in this knowing that I speak to you of.

I have a friend who commented to me once about divine love. His definition of divine love was: to have divine love one must be selfish in our needs to receive what one desires in this world. In my eyes it sounded like he could do anything he wanted without regard to another's feelings. I was hearing him express a selfish physical love. When I first heard him comment, I was confused, as selfishness is not good or divine. It comes from the physical me-me-me state of mind. I didn't understand how he could relate selfishness to divinity. Maybe he was attempting to reason selfishness from a divine state of being. That he was looking out for himself from within, in his wants, needs, dreams and desires.

We must love unconditionally, not selfishly. This is what he may have meant when he said to love himself selfishly. That was a type of unconditional love for him. I love myself so much that I make my decisions from my spirit, not my physical needs and wants. I started to understand what he was saying. To love ourselves so much is to go within to the spirit and ask what our indwelling light spirit wants us to do. What is it that our indwelling spirit wants us to say? Think of a child, a newborn baby. Think of your own children, if you have children. If you do not have children of your own, think of your friends who have children. Or even imagine yourself as a child.

We may find it difficult to figure out if our prayers are coming from the divine or our physical selves. It takes time. It takes time to keep at it, to keep going inside and looking for, searching for, and feeling our spirit. This walk in our life is never ending. We are supposed to keep learning, growing and moving forward. To do this we must consistently look inside of ourselves checking in to find out if we are making decisions from the divine or the selfish. So it is in our prayers. I think this may be why it has been said that "Once the question is asked, the answer is there." All answers are there within us and lie in the universe because we are all one. We all come from the same source, the same Creator. There is no name for our Creator. So don't worry about a name for anything. Just know that our Creator is our Creator. If you are used to using the word *God*, that's fine.

To find out why you praise, consistently go within yourself. Learn some meditation techniques; you could use the meditations I presented to you in chapter thirteen. Use what fits and feels best to you. Stick with it and don't give up. You may also want to take yoga classes. They are all over the place, and there are many different forms of yoga. I want you to have fun with this. Go to classes for many different forms of yoga to find out which one you like best. You may find yourself liking it more than you thought.

It may feel like a chore at first, but once you find something you like, it all becomes easier and more enjoyable. Any time you are in joy, you are close with your spirit. Being close with your spirit will lead you in the right direction always. It opens your mind and body to feeling more. Your eyes will open to see more. Your ears will open to hear more. Your lips will speak more loving care. Love and care about yourself enough to do all of this for you, for when you love you, you give off energy vibrations from above. People around you will feel this and see this. You will start to see and feel more and more from a new light. You will open up everything around you. You will start to live again and become awake.

How Do You Praise?

How do you praise? I ask, how is it that you praise? I can only speak from my own past experiences and what little I know from other people or religions I have read about. When you praise, pray, ask for forgiveness, ask for help, ask for guidance from your higher power, how do you do this? Do you have an altar set up in a special room? Is your space for prayer and worship in your bedroom? In your living room? Downstairs in the basement? Is it outside on your deck? Is it outside under a special tree? Is it just plain ol' outside? Is it in a church you attend? Is it a person to whom you go? Do you praise bowing down or looking up? Do you praise on your knees or with your hands extended above you? Do you praise lying down outside on a blanket under the stars or the sun? Do you lie down on the floor or bed in one of your rooms? Do you sit Indian style with palms up, thumb and index finger together, and tongue pressed to the roof of your mouth? Do you sit cross-legged with palms up in receiving mode? Do you sit with your heels touching like a child? Do you lie curled up on your side in the fetal position? How is your body placed? Where is your body placed? Do you use candles or music? Is your praise in meditation? Is it the meditation?

Meditation can be a way we praise. Meditation can be an added connection or tool in our manner of praise. Many of the methods I listed above are good ways to praise except two of them. Think for a moment about which two you think are not appropriate considering what you have read so far in this book. If you need to go back and reread parts, I invite you to do that now. If you're not sure where to go, where to start first, save this spot and close the book. Lay your hands on top of it, close your eyes, and feel with your hands and heart. Give yourself a good one to three minutes. Then open up the book and without thinking, use one of your hands to mindlessly turn to a page and stop. Read that page or paragraph. Then return back to this page, read the question again, and give your answer.

Now what do you feel? Which two of these recommendations are the inappropriate ones? If you haven't figured it out, I will now tell you. But please, don't jump ahead to the answer. Give yourself the opportunity to answer for yourself. Learn to trust your own instincts. Learn and trust that you can go inside of yourself to the spirit within that guides you, the spirit that knows all source of universal truth.

The two lesser appropriate answers are 1) bowing down and 2) curling up in a ball on your side. The first one, bowing down, is inappropriate and a lie like no other because our Creator is above in the heavens. Never is our Creator, a higher power, ever below us. To bow down is to bow down to slavery/the punisher. That may be harsh to hear or understand or even comprehend, and I will do my best to explain why this is so. I believe the easiest way to explain it is through the mind of a child when speaking to parent—of course making the assumption that the parent is loving and not abusive.

Parents are our guides in life. We look up to them to guide us and give us truth. Similarly, much like a parent is to a child, our Creator is to us, her children seeking truth. So praise up to the sky, the heavens, the stars and the moon, the sun and clouds, the rain in the air. As I've mentioned before, our Creator creates and can only create. All divine beings of light and love are above and from above, never below or under us to bow to. When I was out in the cornfield behind the house where I lived when I was married, I raised my hands to the heavens, asking for guidance, proclaiming I would live my life for my Creator, that I would follow what my Creator saw fit for me to do. Some may think bowing down is a way to express their humbleness. I understand because I grew up in a Roman Catholic family and we bowed (kneeling-bowing heads-similar enough to consider as bowing) many times throughout service. If we really stop to think about this deeper we can see more clearly that bowing down represents slavery; as if our creator owns us. No one owns us. Church does not own you. The man or woman in the pulpit does not own you. The religion you may practice does not own you. The words in church or religious books do not own you, telling you rules, laws and guidelines you MUST follow to be right with God. You own yourself. You take responsibility for yourself. Our Creator gave us the gift of free will. That is the simple beauty of life, of truth. We choose daily what we think, what we do, where we go, with whom we spend time with or not spend time with, how we act and react. We choose literally everything. Many times we make our choices out of fear. Let's now re learn how to better ourselves and love ourselves more fully.

The second action, curling up in a ball on your side, is a symbol of fear or wanting someone to take you away from wherever you are in that moment or thought. We curl up because we feel that we want or need to get away from something or someone. It could also be that we want or need to be close to someone or something outside of us. We may feel a need for someone to take us away from pain that is going on inside of us. It is okay to want to be held and comforted. It is up to us to find balance in all things.

Curling up in a ball on your side could also indicate a feeling of unworthiness or emptiness or loneliness. In this case we feel that we want to crawl back inside our mothers womb so we can be protected, just like I wanted to after each time abuse occurred and after sex with my ex-husband. In the sense of mother/child, this may not be our best choice … to run away back to the comfort of our mothers' wombs, where no one can hurt us, to rely on someone else to take care of us, to rely on someone else to love us, to rely on someone else to protect us, to rely on someone else to take care of all our needs. We need to rely on ourselves. When we need spiritual help, we should call on the Creator, the Angels of Light, or the spirit that lives within us. I know it is easier said than done, but as we desire to grow and become the enlightened person we want to be, we must stay committed to ourselves, stay committed to the promise we made to our Creator.

Sometimes we get confused with the physical and divine. There are times when we might think we are speaking or acting divinely when we are actually speaking and acting from the physical. It is obvious to some, but some actions and words are not so obvious to others. Let me attempt to give you an example or two. I give you these examples from my life, as I can speak only from my life. As I look back on times I thought I was being divine, I now see that I was not. This scenario I give you below took place shortly after I was divorced.

I became involved with a man who had cheated on his first wife and had cheated on his girlfriends. I later found out that I was one of the women he cheated on too. He was definitely a player. You know how women can be sometimes, trying to change the man they are with. Well, I also attempted to do that to this boyfriend using the Bible. I thought at the time that I was helping him. I wanted to help him understand that cheating was wrong and he would pay for his sins when he died, that God was watching him from above and he needed to wake up and be a man; he needed to get with the program.

It didn't matter how many times I explained certain things, he simply did not want to hear it. He was going to do what he wanted to do, and no one was going to stop him. I had used my words in a self-righteous way, expressing to him that he was going to go to hell. I wasn't being divine. I wanted him to change. I wanted him to be the man I knew I deserved. Well, you can't ever make someone change if he or she doesn't want to. You can't force or push someone to change if he or she is not even looking to change in order to make a better life. That person chooses his or her circle of life just like everyone else.

The way in which I did this was not in line with divinity. Plus, I was too fresh out of my marriage. I still had a lot of anger inside me from the marriage and toward my father. My reasons were selfish. I was thinking more about me—what he should do or how he should be in order to please me.

Another incident happened more recently in 2011. I want to mention it to show you that I am still human and make mistakes. We need to not only learn from our mistakes, but even more importantly, we need to not condemn ourselves when we make them. Our mistakes are purely a source from which to learn. Each and every one of them. Never condemn yourself for a mistake; always forgive yourself. We must love and forgive any person when he or she makes a mistake, whether it involved you or not. In order to get out of that person's circle of life, we must love and forgive him or her. Not judge. We are not a judge, convicter, or punisher of any man or woman.

So back to my example. Here I am as a massage therapist, energy goddess, coach, guide, and healer, and I receive an e-mail from a potential new client. He had reached out to me months before, and I had felt something then that said to me, "No, don't." Getting together didn't work out at that time, so I let time pass.

I actually knew this person on a casual basis as one professional to another. I had known him for many years. This time around, I informed him to not have expectations about my service other than that he was going to get a great massage. I explained my work to him in relation to his work, as he is a physical therapist. He is the one who controls how his patients' therapy goes. As the massage therapist, I too direct how my patients' sessions go. I thought he understood that, but apparently he didn't get it, because a few minutes into the session he made inappropriate remarks and suggestions and asked questions that were uncalled for. I reminded him again of protocol, which he ignored. At this point I informed him the session was over and that he needed to leave. He disregarded my request.

I remained calm, cool, and collected. I was firmly within my rights, and he still continued to dishonor and disrespect me. I started to become angry because he was not leaving my home. Now all I wanted was for him to be out of my house. I could not believe this individual was still being disrespectful toward me. In a situation like this, remaining in a divine state was difficult for me. He just wouldn't leave. After he left, he continued his madness by texting me several times. I chose to disregard his messages. My state went from divine to physical within minutes.

Making this story deeper was the fact that I had not obeyed my inner voice when the spirit within me told me at the very beginning, "No, don't see this person." I allowed my physical greed to lead me at the time. I had wanted to meet my financial quota for the week. It was just a bad decision all the way around. If I had followed through with my spirit's advice when it spoke to me the first time, I wouldn't have gotten into the whole mess. Because I knew of my own damage, I cleansed myself and my home with white sage. I forgave myself, and I forgave him, letting it go, releasing it to the Creator to be dealt with. I will let my Creator deal with him. I released any judgment I had toward him, and I got out of his circle. His karma would come back to him eventually. It always does. The truth always comes forth sooner or later. Men always reveal their true selves in time. And when I say *men*, I mean man, as in both men and women.

Whenever, however, and for whatever reason you praise, be careful of everything you do, say, or think. It is all a form of energy. Think on this. Any time you damage your mind, you damage your spirit. Darkness attempts to overtake light. Notice I said it *attempts*. It cannot overtake us if we know we have our white light inside us, which is our angel spirit. We need to know it is there, to recognize it is there. We must use our spirit for our good and the good of all others.

Your physical self or your divine self? Fear or enlightenment? Which do you choose? What is it to be enlightened? What does it take to become enlightened? Enlightenment is a state of fearlessness. How does one become fearless, unafraid of anything, anyone, any circumstance? What must we do right now as we live in these physical bodies to *be* enlightened? What must we learn to come to a state of wanting to be enlightened? Do we feel we must meet a point of desperation before we make this decision? And if so, why? Why not consciously make the choice now to become enlightened? To love ourselves that much. To make our decisions from our divine selves, not out of fear. Fear of the unknown.

Why do we fear the unknown? Is it because we cannot see it? Because we do not know what life holds for us? What is faith? Faith is trusting in the unknown of what our Creator has for us. Trusting that our Creator has plans for us. But does our Creator have plans for us? Or do we make our own plans? Or is it both? We have free will because our Creator gives us free will. Our Creator wants the best for us. But does the Creator want the best for us? How do we love unconditionally? Ask yourselves these questions. I want you to contemplate them. You do the work.

Everything and everyone, animate and inanimate, plants and animals, the ocean and the trees, and even words have vibration. What are you vibrating? What kind of vibrations are you giving out? Where are you vibrating?

Enlightenment—are you on the path to it? You either are or you are not. There is no in between. You are either open or you are not open. You either search to live in truth or you don't. There is only one truth, which is the universal truth, for it would not be considered truth if it were not universal, hence the word *universal*. It does not matter what color or nationality you are. There may be hundreds of different kinds of religion, each with its own belief of what truth is. I must say that universal truth it is not a religion.

Words

Once you start to think about it, the truth is in our words. I believe the word *try* should not even be in the English language, because we don't try something. We are either doing it or not doing it. We don't try to keep our eyes open; they are either closed or open. We don't try to make money; we are either making money or we are not. We do not try to put on a pair of socks. We either are or we are not. We do not try a taste of food. We either will have a bite of it or not. We are not going to try a flavor of something different. We will either taste it or not taste it. We don't try to love ourselves; we either love ourselves or we don't. We do not try to love others; we either love them or we don't. We do not try to spend time with others, such as our loved ones, families, friends, or our most sacred beloveds; we either are spending time with them or we are not. We may be attempting, working, following orders to the best of our ability to do certain things but we don't "try."

The word *try* should not exist! How and why did it ever even get into the English language? We are writing or not writing, eating or not eating, sleeping or not sleeping, cutting our fingernails or not cutting our fingernails. Literally everything we do, think, and say we are doing, thinking, or saying. We are never *not* doing something or not thinking something. Our minds, our brains are constantly functioning every moment we are alive. If you think you are trying, then you are not on the high road of enlightenment.

The good news is that if you fall, because of free will, we have the good choice to get back up. All it takes is humble gratitude. It takes desire. It takes never giving up. It requires consistency and commitment. It requires dedication. It requires loving ourselves enough to do what is required in order for us to reach an enlightened state. Some of these things, which are changes, will not feel pleasant. Change usually isn't comfortable. But once you work through your challenges, it becomes easier and easier.

We are either leading our lives with our spirit or leading our lives with our physical. To be one with our spirit is pure fulfilled joy. To be ruled by our spirit where all truth lives, it can not be fathomed in our minds of what takes place in the divine spiritual realm. This is where faith and trust comes in. It is important we work through *difficult* times, what our mind perceives as difficult times. We are given what we are capable of dealing with. How long must we continue to fight this battle between good and evil? Do you not see? Do you not realize the constant battle we put ourselves through when all we really have to do, and all we really can do, is go within and listen? We become emotional or so unattached from others and ourselves that we forget about others, that they have lives too, just like we have. When we are willing vessels, fear melts off us so we can see the spirit within others.

If we treat our planet, universe, friends, relatives, coworkers, and all other human beings with lack of respect, honor, integrity, and dignity, we have chosen from our free will. When we do this, we are welcoming chaos into our lives. Free will is a gift that our Creator has given us. We use this beautiful gift when we make good and bad decisions. We use our free will when we hate someone or give suffering to someone. We use our free will when we do these things to ourselves. In so doing, we suffer the spiritual consequences of these decisions. Do you see? Let's work on getting out of our Earth boxes and into the spiritual world.

There are no boxes in the spiritual world. We are free to roam wherever we choose once we are out of our bodies and in our spirit. Free will does not stop after our bodies die. The spirit is spirit and lives forever. The spirit has the choice to use free will. Are you a good spirit? Are you a bad spirit? Do you feel stuck somewhere in the middle, going back and forth, not knowing which way to turn? Are you in a constant state of sitting on the fence? What is going on inside your mind right now? Are you thinking, *Oh what a dilemma*? It's not really a dilemma unless we make it one, because here we go again, using our free will to make it a dilemma.

We make choices all the time, every single day. Every time you do something or don't do something, every time you say something or don't say something, every thought you have, every act you make is a decision. From the time you open your eyes in the morning until you fall asleep at night, you are making decisions. Love you enough to see the spirit space inside you. This spirit inside you is all love; it loves you unconditionally. And it is a safe place.

CHAPTER 16

Angel Speaks

A Dream

One evening in the early part of the year of 2010, my Angel Bearer of Light spoke to me about a dream he'd had the night before. He informed me that he rarely dreams, but when he does, there is a deep spiritual significance to them. In his dream, spirits spoke to him, letting me know that I was to write a book. I had never expressed to him anything about my desire to one day write about my life. It was very exciting for me to know this information.

It was years ago, back in the 1990s, that I had a very dear friend with whom I met three days a week to exercise. One of the days we got together, she expressed to me that she thought it would be a good idea for me to one day write a book about my life. She could see how much of an inspiration I could be for others.

I had always known that at some point in my life there would come a time when I would want to write a book, but I never quite knew when or how it would take place. So when my angel spoke to me of this, I was even more eager to start the process, even if it was only to start thinking more about it. But before I could write, much healing needed to take place in me first. It was on April 11, 2011 that I began the writing of this book.

I would like to preface the following passage. First of all I have lived in fear most of my life. As a child growing up in a negative home with a father sexually abusing me to marrying a man who was controlling and abusive spiritually, emotionally, mentally, and sexually, I carried with me fear. It was years gone by before I could start to learn to become free. It had taken me a long time to reach a place of love and forgiveness towards my father and ex-husband. The requirements were for me to not only learn some universal truths but to love and forgive myself first before being able to love and forgive others. It is impossible to truly love and forgive others without having love and forgiveness for ourselves first. When I had moments of fear I used the dreams within my mind and heart as courage to overcome the many obstacles I encountered during my life. I am excited to now share the following with you that my Angel Bearer of Light specifically said to me about me. It is my desire that your mind, body, and life become free so you will reach enlightenment. Here you go:

YOUR DEEPEST FEAR IS NOT THAT YOU ARE INADEQUATE BUT THAT YOU ARE POWERFUL BEYOND MEASURE. IT IS YOUR OWN LIGHT THAT FRIGHTENS YOU MOST. ACTING OUT SMALL DOESN'T SERVE YOUR SELF OR OTHERS, FOR THERE IS NOTHING ENLIGHTENING ABOUT ACTING SO. SHRINKING SO THAT OTHER PEOPLE AND FRIENDS AROUND YOU WON'T FEEL INSECURE WILL ONLY CREATE FEAR. ALL WERE CREATED PURE AND MEANT TO SHINE AS CHILDREN. THE LIGHT OF CREATION IS NOT JUST IN SOME BUT IN ALL! AND AS YOU LET YOUR OWN LIGHT SHINE, YOU WILL SPIRITUALLY SIGNAL TO OTHERS PERMISSION TO DO THE SAME. AS YOU ARE FREED OF YOUR OWN FEARS YOUR EXAMPLE HELPS OTHERS TO SEE THEIR OWN FEARS AND BECOME FREED OF THEIR FEARS AS WELL. FROM THIS WILL COME THE WORLD OF ENLIGHTENMENT!

Telling My Mom Who

It was January 17, 2012, when I went to inform my mom who my perpetrator was. I had been thinking about it for a time and it had recently resurfaced. As I neared the completion of this book, I knew letting my mom know the identity of the perpetrator of my childhood abuse was important to me for many reasons. It was important for my own spiritual growth. It was important for me because I knew that if I did not face this, I would ultimately be the one to suffer the consequences.

Becoming fearless in going forward with this news was important for my future, in the work I would be doing. I knew more blessings would come because of my fearlessness. Freedom comes to me in every aspect of my life. It was not a personal vendetta. Holding this information inside of my body was causing me pain. My head hurt. My stomach was in knots. My ability to keep grounded was off. My thinking and creative abilities were limited. This pain was on my mind so much that I was having difficulty functioning. If I had allowed this to manifest inside me, I would have ultimately delivered myself a disease of some kind.

The origins of some of our diseases come from pent up, built up emotional scars. These emotional scars can become physical scars. Some people cut themselves, some eat their hair, some deal with their hurt emotions through drugs, food, alcohol, body piercings, eating plastic, the need to constantly have something in their mouth, getting tattoos—many different forms of physical degradation of the body. It all starts with our thoughts and how we think about ourselves, the way we have been treated, the way we were brought up. Many factors are involved, but all things start with thought and our actions and reactions to stimuli, both our own and those of others.

When I felt the urgency to tell my mother the news of who my perpetrator was, I was scared. But I knew this had to be done. When I called her to make sure she was home before I drove over, my anxiety rose. I cried. I sobbed. When I arrived at my mom's, I wanted to search through old photos first. Hours passed with me still holding this information in. I had already told my Angel Bearer of Light I was going to see my mom. My angel helped me fight through my pain. He helped me know and believe

I could do this. I knew my angel was right, yet I was still frightened. I didn't want to hurt my mom with any of my words. Yet at the same time I knew I *had* to do this for me.

My mom was preparing dinner when my angel told me, "Sure, you can. Of course it is important to tell her." I felt I couldn't do it, saying, "I don't think it's going to happen today." My angel informed me, "Then quit the book now. No fear. No hypocrites." My angel went on to say, "If you cannot tell your mom, but you can tell the world, then you must quit or be fearless and push forward." I said to my angel, "I will not quit the book!"

Knowing the importance of my writings, knowing I had my angel with me all of the time, knowing my strength, courage, and spiritual powers were great, I could not and would not fall back now! The time had come for me to do this. I loved my mom. She gave me life. She cared for me and loved me every step of my life.

I broke out into tears, went to her, and let her know I needed to talk. She immediately came to my side, and we sat down. I started my conversation by letting her know how much I loved her and didn't want to hurt her. I expressed that I needed to tell her about something from my past, something that had happened a long time ago. She listened with love. I reminded her of the time I came to her and told her I had to stop cleaning her house, and she remembered this. I went on, explaining that it had been Dad who sexually abused me. I saw her pain.

She wanted to know if I had told anyone else. I let her know that I had. I told her the kids knew. I told her I'd had conversations with two of my sisters and one of my brothers. I gave her my perceptions of each one of my siblings. She was amazed at my perceptions because she agreed and saw them as accurate. Remember, I am the sixth child out of seven. I wanted her to know this information was going to be in my book and that she deserved to hear it straight from me and no one else.

My mom has always seen strength and determination in me. She was sorry and didn't know what to say. I let her know that it was okay and that if she ever wanted to talk to me or had questions, I was there for her. I told her, "I am fine, Mom. I will be fine. I have been fine." I told my mom I had known I needed to have love and forgiveness toward my dad before he died and how easy it had been to love him as he was dying in hospice care at home. She seemed to understand more.

Facing Our Fears

Going through this was difficult, but it was a huge, freeing experience to finally let it out. It is important for every single one of us to face our fears—our emotional, mental, and spiritual fears—for if we do not do this, we will never be free. You can believe in Jesus, Krishna, Buddha, and all of the great teachers of our time, but if you cannot release yourself from the bondage that holds you down, you will never have total peace, love, forgiveness, and spiritual freedom. We must love all. We must forgive all. We must love ourselves and forgive ourselves at all times. No one is exempt from this. All of the great teachers have said the truth sets us free. They also have said the truth can be troubling to us, but through the trouble we are free at last.

I see more of what my angel was telling me. Spirits speak to my angel, and my angel in human form speaks to me. Everything is given to me for a reason. Truth lives within our spirit, which is inside these bodies we carry around. How many of us know that we carry a spiritual being inside of us? How many know this light within us is a spirit—a white light spirit? It is a pure, vibrant energy.

We have been neglecting these lives of ours for way too long. When will be your day of opening to this brilliant white light? When will you stop hiding behind your hands or your voice or your sight or your hearing? When will you make this stand for spiritual freedom? You are the only one who can make this decision. The more walls you break down, the freer you become. Angels know when someone has done his or her very best. Then it comes to a person to know that he or she has. It will become that person's destiny. Always be honest to your spirit about whatever it is! To put something off that is spiritually important will affect your personal power.

I will no longer hide. I am honored to be chosen for such work. It is a privilege and great responsibility. I love my hands. I love my voice. I love my light. I love all Angels of Light.

About the Author

Barbara Anne Rose is a loving mother of three grown children: Matthew, Jeffrey, and Kelly. She has been an inspiration to hundreds of men and women throughout her adult life, helping people to change their bodies, open their minds, and enlighten their spirits. She has taught exercise to seniors and volunteered her time with those less fortunate. She continues to inspire many men and women through exercise, nutrition, and spiritual fearlessness.

Barbara has had the privilege to be a part of many speaking engagements at churches, businesses, and schools. She has also been featured as a fitness model in magazines and interviewed by newspapers. Two of her works involved television.

Barbara has always had a passion to serve others. This is her first published work.

Barbara is a licensed massage therapist living and practicing in the state of Delaware. She is NCBTMB (National Certification Board for Therapeutic Massage and Bodywork) with emphasis on spiritual healing.

Look for more upcoming books by Barbara Anne Rose based on relationships, exercise and nutrition and spirituality infused with angel teachings throughout.

To contact her, you can reach her through one of her websites:

- www.goddessoftherose.com
- www.spiritualhealingmassage.com
- www.barbaraannerose.com

Index

180